HEAR MY SILENCE

HEAR MY SILENCE

SURVIVING DEPRESSION

Karina Colgan

POOLBEG

Published 2008
by Poolbeg Press Ltd
123 Grange Hill, Baldoyle
Dublin 13, Ireland
E-mail: poolbeg@poolbeg.com

© Karina Colgan 2008

The moral right of the author has been asserted.

Typesetting, layout, design © Poolbeg Press Ltd.

1 3 5 7 9 10 8 6 4 2

A catalogue record for this book is available from the British Library.

ISBN 978-1-84223-367-2

Typeset by Patricia Hope

Printed by
CPI Cox & Wyman, Reading RG1 8EX

www.poolbeg.com

Both author and publisher wish the reader to know that this book does not offer or constitute professional medical advice. The identities of the people written about in this book have been disguised to afford their right to privileged communication with the author.

About the author

Karina Colgan lives in south Dublin. She has worked as a journalist for the past fifteen years and as a magazine publisher for six. She is the bestselling author of *You Have to Scream with Your Mouth Shut: Violence in the Home* and *If It Happens To You: Miscarriage and Stillbirth – A Human Insight.* She is currently working on her next book about the organ retention scandal in Ireland, which will be published by Poolbeg Press in 2009. You can e-mail Karina at: **hearmysilence@eircom.net**

Acknowledgements

I would like to start by saying that writing a book like this impacts many people for different reasons, not least the author's family and friends. They are the ones who lived through my hellish nightmare and were forced to watch helplessly as I spiralled out of control. I know that without their love and support this book would not have been possible and it is for this reason that I acknowledge them first. To my two beloved children Karl and Sarah, who saw my darkest days and loved me despite them. Know how very proud I am of you – you are my greatest achievements and I love you both so very much. To my mother Christina, who has always been there with love, support, and advice, not to mention words of wisdom, reassurance, and literary advice. To my sister Tammy, you know all that you have done and how very grateful I will always be – you are, truly, a sis in a million. To my friends and, in particular, Anna, who lived through it with me and constantly cracked the whip as I was writing this book. To Lorraine, who didn't give up on me, despite months of no contact and her many calls and texts going unanswered; to E O'D for his support and advice for well over a decade.

Finally, I reserve my biggest thanks for Gerry, a man who loves and supports me unconditionally and the person who saved me. There are few men like you, Gerry, and I thank you from the bottom of my heart. This one's for you.

I would also like to extend my thanks to: John Lonergan, Governor, Mountjoy Prison; Sandra Hogan, PRO, Aware; Rachel Van Hoven, Information Officer, Aware; Dr James Lee, Director, Primacare Group. To the many healthcare professionals who assisted me in Ireland, Europe, Canada and the USA, too numerous to mention; you know who you are and how thankful I am. To Ruth Killeen; Martin O'Hara; Patricia Fox; Madge Fogarty, Post Natal Depression Ireland; National Office for Suicide Prevention; Phil DiRosa, CAMH, Canada; Michel Aarden, The Netherlands; Jed Diamond, USA; Norman Slack; Andy Sargent; L. Armstrong; and Nicola Fox, who is practically a part of the family and a student of journalism. Nicola was a great help to me in getting surveys and questionnaires completed. It would be remiss to conclude my acknowledgements without mentioning Kieran Devlin, Paula Campbell, and the rest of the team at Poolbeg Press, and finally to my editor, Brian Langan, who by now, probably knows this book as well as I do.

Dedication

To the most precious thing in my life; my family: Gerry, Karl, Sarah and Glen Colgan (RIP); my mother Christina; my sister Tammy and nephews Sam, Owen, Mark and Paul. Also to Anna C, Tanya-Samantha who will never be forgotten, and my great-grandfather, Joseph Charles Hawe, for giving me his passion of writing.

Contents

Introduction

"The most violent element in society is ignorance."

EMMA GOLDMAN

Depression is like an invasive cancer that grips every aspect of your very being and drags you into an emotional whirlpool and apathetic abyss. It renders you helpless and eats away at every last vestige of your self-worth and self-esteem. It is an illness that takes many by surprise, often because their breaking point has been reached many times before they finally succumb and go under. I acknowledge that my story is shocking, but every story of depression is devastating to those affected by it, both directly and indirectly.

Statistics show that 400,000 people in Ireland suffer from depression at any given time. Add to that the average of five people who will be impacted by every single case and a further 450-plus people who take their own lives every year (80 per cent of all suicides can be attributed to depression) and the figures make horrific reading.

Sadly these figures only represent the reported cases. Many more cases go unreported for fear of being "labelled" or "stigmatised" and the true extent of Ireland's hidden epidemic and silent suffering may never truly be known. I am of the opinion – and several research studies support my opinion – that depression is Ireland's biggest social problem. Research shows that three out of four people hide it from work colleagues and employers. Women are, on average, almost four times more likely than men to suffer with depression, but men are far more likely to die by suicide. Depression plays a very large role in over 450 deaths by suicide every year. A staggering one in four men and one in two women will suffer from depression at some stage in their lives, whether episodic or sustained, and many of these people will keep it quiet and refrain from seeking help or telling anyone because of the "shame". Stigma can – and does – take lives and also stops people from getting the help that they so desperately need.

Thankfully, I was never suicidal; I just wanted to escape my hellish nightmare and to feel the terrible weight that burdened my every waking moment float away for a while. I just didn't want to exist, though the thought of killing myself never entered my head. Retrospectively, it was little short of a miracle that I did not die during the final months of my breakdown, for I diced with death many times.

In the year leading up to my meltdown, some days the effort of trying to decide what to eat and get up was so overwhelming I went without. For weeks at a time I stayed in bed, moving only when I absolutely had to. I withdrew from life as depression cast its veil over me and at times, the effort of breathing was so exhausting, it reduced me to a Beckett-like elegiac presence in the bed.

For those who have never suffered from depression, it can be difficult to understand how simple, everyday tasks become monumental decisions for a depressed and often apathetic person. When the effort of getting up is so great, you don't. My phone went unanswered and my post went unopened. You shut down, pushing those who love you most away. I felt like I was living in a fog; an empty place devoid of emotional or intellectual stimulation, a place without rationality or reason that was littered with incipient apathy. At times my emotional pain was joined by physical pain – like there was a blockage in my chest that threatened to suffocate me. At times my heart beat so erratically I thought it would burst through my ribcage.

Apathy washed over me to the point where I had no interest in anybody or anything. Retrospectively, I know that I put my family through hell, but that is the nature of the beast that is depression. At first you try to cover it up because you are perceived as this strong and capable person and to admit weakness would be seen as failure; a moral flaw, a character imperfection that would bring shame. However, there comes a point when depression has such a grip on you that is impossible to hide it, but by then it doesn't really matter, because you no longer care what people think.

As someone used to being in control, failure was not a word in my vocabulary. I was a born leader. I was the rock upon which so many people climbed and there were days well before my meltdown when I wanted to scream, "What about me?" I never did though. Living in a society that – wrongly in my opinion – equates success with happiness, I was seen as the successful wife, mother, career woman, author, friend, employer, businesswoman, neighbour . . . the list goes on. I was the stereotypical example of a woman who "had it all". I had the house, the car, the children, the marriage, the dog, the company and professional recognition for my work. This perception couldn't have been further from the truth. In the space of three years, I lurched from one major crisis to another, which landed me in hospital a number of times with stress-related problems including, among other things, two suspected heart-attacks; pleurisy; irritable bowel syndrome; surgeries and also the complicated removal of my gallbladder.

I remember lying in hospital after one surgery; I was hooked up to morphine and fluid drips. In one hand I had a button to control pain relief, in the other my mobile phone. I couldn't move with the pain, but I was trying to deal with problems at the office from my hospital bed and come up with a solution that would save my company. I never found it, but I spent a further two years looking and getting further into debt. The end of my business was the death of my dream and it hit me hard. I went into liquidation three days before Christmas. That day was the start of a depression that would increase in severity for the next twelve months, culminating in a four-month period of complete meltdown.

I was intellectually astute enough to know what was happening from my work as a journalist and also the fact that I graduated in a psychology-related field, but I wasn't a psychopathologist. I remember walking into my doctor's office one day and telling him that I was having a breakdown. Having seen me go through so many traumas and bounce back, I don't think at first he really understood the enormity of what I was saying to him. I wasn't going to bounce back this time. In fact, I felt like I was freefalling into an abyss so deep it would quickly swallow me.

The treatments for depression were mostly not for me. I was sceptical of anti-depressants, became dependent on sleeping tablets and, as a very private person, counselling was a definite no-no. Apart from my family, much of my journey through depression was shared with a close friend, also a journalist, who cajoled and eventually threatened me with unmentionable things if I did not write about my experience.

Having lived through this illness and fortunately emerged the other side of it, I am appalled and angry that in a country as progressive as Ireland, stigma and a glaring lack of public expenditure to provide information, treatment and support remain serious problems for those afflicted by depression. This is an issue that urgently needs to be addressed. More funds need to be made available to channel into education, advertising and support mechanisms. Not every person suffering from depression has the luxury of private healthcare. Sadly, like many other "progressive" countries, Ireland has a two-tier healthcare system, where those who receive public healthcare are just part of a faceless public system and have to wait months – often in a crisis situation – to get help and support. They are mere numbers on increasingly long waiting lists. As I discovered from speaking to people when writing this book, some are forced to borrow money to avail of services such as counselling and psychotherapy because they are not in a position where they can wait months to get treatment, either for themselves or for a loved one.

There is no one cause of depression; indeed the numerous possible causes make it a continuum. Depression is international; it crosses all social, religious, cultural, economic and political divides and it is not more prevalent in any one background. It is often (but not always) triggered after a setback in life such as financial worries; breakdown of a relationship; bereavement; loss of job; or ill health. I suffered all of these in rapid succession, plus the additional trauma of my home burning to the ground, before I reached breaking point and finally went under. I got tired struggling and my brain just switched off. I'd lie in bed for weeks at a time knowing what was wrong, but being powerless to do anything about it.

In my darkest days all I wished for was mundane normality. To be able to do simple everyday things like go to the shops, watch a movie with my daughter, read a book. As a voracious reader, not having the concentration to be able to read was soul-destroying, as was not being able to write or even properly articulate how I was feeling. It took months for me to recover, but I do remember standing in a supermarket one day and feeling on top of the world because I had managed to get up, get washed, get dressed, get out and do the shopping. I am sure that I was a sight to behold as I walked around the aisles grinning with delight. A very insignificant event, you may think, but to someone who has been reclusive and severely depressed, it is a great achievement and a giant step on the road to recovery.

These days, advertisements for road safety abound. While I fully support and endorse such advertisements given the huge number of people killed on our roads each year, there needs to be more recognition and a far greater awareness that depression claims even *more* lives every year. If, as a society, we are to save lives, then it is time to eradicate the stigma. The many professionals who contributed to this book also share this sentiment.

The figures for depression are frightening, yet, despite being Ireland's greatest social problem, it would appear that it is not yet considered to be an urgent "social issue" by Government. Depression is commonly referred to as the "lonely" disease because it leaves people feeling isolated, vulnerable, embarrassed, and despairing. In researching this book, I carried out my own surveys in various places and with various age groups. The results mirrored numerous other studies and surveys and showed a misinformed public with a distinct lack of awareness about depression and driven by stigma.

I believe that this is not through ignorance *per se*, but through a lack of education, readily available information, easily accessible support mechanisms, and positive and sustained advertising. I know from writing this book that many people don't know where to go for help, and when they do finally seek help, many have to wait months for treatment. I was recently in my doctor's surgery where I counted twenty-four different leaflets on display explaining every illness you can think of, with the exception of depression. One must question why.

It is not easy to write a book like this, to lay bare your darkest moments and allow people almost voyeuristic access to your very private world. If it were, then such a book would have been written long ago. This alone clearly demonstrates the stigma surrounding depression. To write it anonymously would serve only to perpetuate the ignorance of stigma. A recent survey by the National Office for Suicide Prevention (NOSP) about awareness and attitudes to depression in Ireland shows that, as a depressed person, I am considered by some people to be a "dangerous person" from whom they should be "protected". One-third of them admitted they would find it difficult to talk to "someone like me". One in four believed I shouldn't be allowed to hold down a responsible job and two-thirds of them, if they had depression, would be prepared to suffer in silence because of the shame they would feel. One can only assume they are unaware of the many psychiatrists, scientists, doctors, neurosurgeons, writers, inventors, academics, physicists, CEOs, intellectuals, law enforcers, pilots, barristers and judges who suffer from depression, or the other famous brilliant minds that feature in Chapter 13 of this book.

One of the most eminent professors of psychiatry and foremost authorities on depressive illness in the world, Kay Redfield Jamison, has written numerous bestsellers and research papers on depression. She is also a manic-depressive, who suffered from this illness while pursuing a career in academic medicine. International educator on depression, psychotherapist Jed Diamond, has written seven books and conducted numerous studies into depression. In fact, he contributes to this book. Again, Jed suffered from depression himself for years. There can be little doubt that ignorance incites fear, and a lack of education influences views as radical as those above. However, that matters little to the hundreds of thousands of people who suffer from depression. Welcome to the stigma that abounds in twenty-first-century Ireland.

I am indebted to those who filled in questionnaires, to the sufferers and their families who spoke so openly and honestly to me and to the professionals who gave so freely of their time and expertise. I know that this book won't solve the problem of depression and I have far from elucidated all the reasons for it, or indeed the causes of it. Nor am I naïve enough to think it will banish stigma or misconception. However, as somebody who has been there, what I hope it will do is to provide an insight into the illness that is depression and to show those who are affected by it that they are not alone.

*Karina Colga*n
May 2008

1

Karina's Story

PROLOGUE

**"Who looks outside dreams,
who looks inside awakens."**

CARL JUNG

This book was prompted by a very dark period in my life and, as such, shows me as a person only during this time. I wasn't always the inept emotional and physical wreck my illness turned me into. In fact, I was very much the opposite.

I was born into a middle-class home in the late 1960s. My sister was born four years later and completed our small family. My mother, who is an extremely intelligent and gifted woman, stayed at home when we were children. As an artist, she was able to pick and choose her commissions and, even then, left working until we both started school. Unlike many mothers today, myself included, she was in the enviable position of not having to work. She is one of those rare people whom everybody loves and who has no enemies. She devoted her life to my sister and I, instilling in us the belief that we could achieve anything we wanted if we put our minds to it. She loved my father deeply until the day he dropped dead while talking to someone at work, and I am sure he loved her.

My father was an intelligent and professional man, who, I believe, was too set in his ways when he married at the age of forty-three to adapt properly to family life. We never wanted for anything materially, but giving us time was not something that came easily to him. Looking back, he struggled enormously with family life, with emotion and with love. It was only after his death, while clearing things, that I found my first book, which he had painstakingly wrapped in tissue and cellophane, along with scrapbooks of press cuttings about the book. Although I was twenty-eight at the time, going through his things made me feel like a child on a voyage of discovery. My memory of this time had been my father commenting that the launch was on at a terribly "inconvenient time". Sadly, it wasn't until I was well into adulthood with children of my own, that I understood he simply didn't know how else to behave.

I was educated privately during my formative years and as a teenager spent most summers in Europe with my mother and sister. These were carefree times with days that were spent learning of cultures, of languages, of new cuisines and of life. My love of words was apparent from an early age. I kept journals and diaries meticulously and I was always driven, determined and inquisitive. I carried a notebook and pen everywhere as a child and while friends got dolls for Christmas, I asked for writing sets and typewriters. I used to read a page of the dictionary every night and my love of words is as strong today as it was then. My great-grandfather wrote for the *Irish Independent* for many years and I believe it is from him that I inherited my passion and love for writing. However, I have endeavoured to live my life according to a verse my grandfather wrote in an autograph book of mine when I was seven: "*Good, better, best; never let it rest, until your good is better, and your better is best.*"

My career as a journalist has spanned almost two decades and I suppose I can be described as somewhat successful insofar as I am a bestselling author and I get paid to do something I love. I have written for most national newspapers and magazines and, for six years, ran my own very busy publishing company employing a large staff.

I enjoy good wine, food, non-fiction books and psychology. I love travelling and seize every opportunity I can to jump on a plane! Thankfully I have a friend who likes to do this as much as I do. Apart from being a great travelling companion, she and I are very alike in temperament, which means we get on well and, as we share a profession, we never run out of things to talk about! We always tend to book another trip as soon as we return from one, to counteract the gloom of having to come back to reality. They are generally months apart, but we thoroughly enjoy counting down the months, then the weeks, the days and eventually, the hours, like excited kids. . . . By the time we meet in the airport, you would be forgiven for thinking we are two fugitives on the run, such is our rush to get on the plane! These trips, coupled with family breaks, just about satisfy my travelling bug, though I still suspect I should have been born in a hot country, which I put down to the little bit of Italian blood I have in me, courtesy of some distant relative!

I confess to being a total news junkie and I simply cannot imagine a world without Sky News, documentaries, current affairs programmes or newspapers. This said, I have a propensity for junk food, chocolate, drinking half cans of Coca-Cola (who drinks flat Coke?), sparkling water, cold coffee, fresh flowers – lilies being my favourite – reality television and soppy movies. I also absolutely love Vimrod (I'm not explaining, but you *really* should Google him)! Did I say I love chocolate? I don't exercise nearly as often as I should and I fail dismally when it comes to eating the recommended serving of five portions of fruit and vegetables daily. However, in my defence, I drink a lot of water and I have recently acquired a smoothie maker, which proves intent.

When it comes to music, I was not blessed with a great singing voice. However, this doesn't stop me singing along to any song I know at the top of my voice, mostly to the horror of my daughter, Sarah, who is an extremely gifted and talented performer! I am caught in a time warp when it comes to music and I am a self-confessed seventies junkie; there are few songs I don't know from this era. I am the proud owner of a DS Lite that I was given for Mother's Day. I am pleased to say, to those "in the know", that my brain age is consistently a very healthy twenty. I am also very partial to Sudoku.

Although I have a rather dry and sometimes dark sense of humour, I can generally laugh at most things. I tend to be a little cynical, which I largely put down to my background of investigative journalism and studies, rather than my nature. Conversely, I have great empathy with people and often wear my heart on my sleeve. I am fiercely protective of, and loyal to, those I love and care about.

I have a wonderful family comprising my husband, two children, mother, sister and four nephews, who eagerly watched the pages of the manuscript for this book increase every time they were over visiting. My godson, Sam (9), gave me a jelly bear figure, and he put it on my desk so it could give me "inspiration" if I needed it. His brothers, identical twins Owen and Mark (7), and Paul (5) also "helped" by giving me some really great ideas . . . mainly about football! Their excitement about the prospect of seeing their names in the book was infectious, so, boys, I kept my promise!

My children are my life's greatest achievements and, like any parent, I am very proud of the adults they have become. While Karl (21) is very laid-back and content to let things happen, Sarah (16) is driven and likes to make things happen. She has a certificate in sign language and is taking Japanese as an additional subject for her Leaving Certificate. She is also a gifted performer and talented singer, and has been a student at a very prestigious music academy for the past three years. Sarah wants to go into psychology and Karl plans a career in counselling, specialising in drug rehabilitation for young people.

My husband, Gerry, is one of the most compassionate, genuinely good, and most caring people on earth. He has great strength and wisdom, and I don't think I have every come across anyone like him. I know that if it were not for him, my story would have been entirely different. In times of great adversity, he remained a constant support and it was his decision to take control that undoubtedly brought me back from the brink. He never judged or blamed me, and I will always be grateful to him.

I am also an extremely private person, which is one of the things that made writing this book and putting myself under such a glaring and (what I imagine will be) subjective spotlight, quite astonishing. I've learned many of life's lessons the hard way and I have been far too trusting at times, particularly in business. However, that's the person I am and I wouldn't change that for a minute. Depression saw me acting in certain ways out of sheer frustration and eventually desperation. I don't think I ever felt as alone in my life as I did during my illness. I like to think of myself as a fighter, but experience has taught me that, eventually, even the strongest person falls and struggles to get up again; becomes too hopeless to hope.

Before my illness I would have considered myself invincible. I got knocked down and I got up again, time after time. So much so, my sister and I used to sing the song that goes "I get knocked down, but I get up again" as the signature tune of every big problem I faced. I was known for battling the odds and for refusing to give up. I used to make light of major crises and prided myself on my ability to overcome adversity, when most other people would have conceded defeat. I remember standing in the shell of my burned-out home and saying to an insurance man that I really didn't have time for this to happen. Although retrospectively I was probably in shock, I was quite serious, because there was a major crisis in the office that also demanded my attention. In the years preceding my battle with depression, I lurched from one major crisis to another without pausing for breath. Every time I was struck down with a stress-related illness, I would convince myself something else was to blame, contrary to what doctors or surgeons told me.

Depression is a deeply lonely disease; it is isolating and it snatches away your ability to interact or communicate with other people, even those who are closest to you. However, of all the symptoms of depression, loneliness is one of the easiest symptoms for other people to identify with; there are few people on this earth who have not experienced loneliness at some point in their lives. However, most of the symptoms of depression are difficult for non-depressed people to relate to and there remains a distinct undercurrent of belief that depressed people "wallow" in their illness, which, of course, science, biology and medical research prove to be completely untrue. Depression is a deeply debilitating illness, which turns the sufferer into a person unrecognisable from their former self and causes them to behave in a manner that is often completely out of character. I know there were many times when my behaviour frightened others and terrified me. Feelings of shame, worthlessness and self-loathing are common.

For me, denial was the first emotion. The last was complete resignation. This person I didn't recognise, and who repulsed me, had replaced the person I knew myself to be. I used what little strength I had left to rebel against it at first. Every time depression reared its ugly head I would shoot it down. I stumbled through the year before the final months of my meltdown with varying degrees of competency. It is difficult to lose everything you know and not be affected by it, but I believed it to be possible.

17

I was the last person my decline became apparent to, even though I was the first to recognise that I was in the process of being dragged into a place I had no idea how to get out of. I should have stopped at that point and sought help, but shame and embarrassment stopped me and instead I stumbled my way through another few months. I now know why depression is such an unreported illness. My world was getting darker and the ritual of getting up eventually became too much. Not long after that, the ritual that was life also became too much, so my mind suspended it and shut down.

Strangely enough, I never wallowed in self-pity; I only blamed myself for being weak. Of course, this wasn't the case, but I didn't know this at the time. Towards the end, even sleeping pills stopped working, taking away the only escape I had. Interestingly – for I have analysed it myself many times – when I was in an almost trance-like state from sleeping pills I would lie in bed and send gibberish texts and voicemails, believing that they made complete sense. Of course they didn't, but retrospectively, I believe that, at these times, in my subconscious, I was screaming out for the help I resisted in my consciousness.

Being the strong and determined person I usually was, many people simply didn't know how to react to me, including my family initially. Some friends chose to pretend nothing was wrong, some stayed out of contact, and many maintained occasional contact. Two didn't give up, despite every effort they made to communicate going un-acknowledged. There are other people I know, however, who will read my story and their jaws will hit the floor with shock, for they know me only as a strong, capable, serious and professional person. Finally, there are those who will read my story and know their contribution to my illness.

It took a series of events for Gerry and my family to forcibly intervene after many months of me shutting them out. Gerry saved me both from myself and from the vice-grip of depression, and he and the rest of my family proved a powerful amulet against the difficulties of my sometimes arduous, and always challenging, journey back to normality. When you are depressed, you don't want to see people. You don't want to go out and you don't have the energy or inclination to shake yourself down and get on with life. The consequences don't matter. There is little point telling a depressed person to "snap out of it" or to "pull themselves together". They cannot. They are in a world that is so dark, it is impossible for them to see the smallest ray of light. It is easy to give up on a depressed person or to adopt the attitude that they will contact you when they are ready to. I can tell you it doesn't work like this. You are encouraging the depression by leaving them alone. They won't ring you; I switched my phone off. You may not be thanked at the time for constantly intruding on their preferred world of isolation but, I assure you, their thanks will come later.

I won't pretend that recovery from depression is easy. It is not. Depression is ugly, it's invasive, it's destructive, it's debilitating, it's consuming and it's utterly soul-destroying. At first, it pushes you to your limits, and when you exceed them, it sends you plummeting into a vortex of emotional despair. It punctures, it wounds, it scars your emotional landscape and it is unrelenting in its evisceration of your life. Its pain and devastation are unimaginable, unless, of course, you have seen them for yourself.

I had to accept that I was depressed before I could understand it and I had to learn to deal with it before I could truly recover from it. It was a vicious circle and a very ambivalent time, which saw me alternate between raw emotion and clinical detachment. Eventually, there came a time when I was able to remove myself from the situation and observe it like a dispassionate onlooker. I took on the role of a researcher, yet I still couldn't elucidate answers. However, the more I learned, the more I began to understand it, and the less I blamed myself: this was not my fault, nor was it a personal weakness. It was something that one in four people suffer from, and most certainly, nothing to be ashamed of.

You have to learn to forget the person that was and concentrate on the person that is. Re-entry to normal life is not something that happens overnight. However, what I can tell you is, it *does* happen. Learning to believe in yourself and your capabilities again is not easy when you have come from the depths of despair. However, slowly the realisation dawns that nothing is so bad that it cannot be overcome and that you have a lot to offer as a person.

My story is told in loose chronological form for the purpose of condensing it for this book. I have not gone into every detail of every incident, for there were far too many – some worse than those I have chosen to highlight in this book. This is primarily because I am conscious of my family's feelings and also of their right to privacy. Many of the major traumas in my life are each worthy of books in their own right and one day, I may well write them.

THE ROAD TO DEPRESSION

**"We don't see things as they are.
We see them as we are."**

ANAÏS NIN

I remember a bang, seeing something white and then a lot of noise. I don't have any memories from the next few days, probably as a result of banging my head. Apparently, the loud noise I heard was in fact the fire brigade cutting me out of my car and the white thing I remembered was my airbag, which activated upon impact. I am told it was a four-car pile-up and that it took quite a while for the fire brigade to cut the roof off my car and get me out. My car was a complete write-off and I sustained various injuries. I attribute this event as a defining point in my life. It was as if someone had switched a light on in my dark world of depression, in which I had existed, not lived, for the previous fourteen months.

As someone who had always been successful, focused, in control and independent, depression hit me like a tidal wave and engulfed me so deeply, I didn't think I would ever claw my way out. It engulfed every single aspect of my life and attacked every one of my cognitive processes. It put my life on hold, threw me into an emotional limbo and its ramifications were enormous – emotionally, physically and financially. Although my final four-month meltdown was a year in the making, I know that the seeds of depression were planted many years before. . . .

The death of my son

On 12 January 1990, my son, Glen, was stillborn. I had been in hospital for bed-rest and on the day of my discharge I went for a routine scan. Later that day a nurse came to tell me that I had to go for another scan. I remember joking with her, saying, "It must be a very good-looking baby!" When we arrived at the scan room, the doctor who had looked after me throughout my pregnancy was already there. The moment I saw her I knew that something was wrong and I felt my mouth go dry. As I sat facing her I didn't realise quite how bad things were. My initial thought was that she was going to suggest that I should remain in hospital because of my back.

She gently told me that there was something seriously wrong with the baby and advised that I wait until my husband arrived before we went any further. My first reaction was to burst into tears. My second was terror. I kept saying, "Melody is going to live, isn't she?" I was convinced the baby was a girl at this point. When the doctor didn't dispel my fears, the realisation dawned that my baby could die. I panicked and remember saying to the doctor that she couldn't let anything happen to the baby I had waited so long for. She squeezed my arm and said that I was to page her the minute my husband arrived.

I left the room in a complete daze and made an almost incoherent telephone call to my husband and then another to my mother. Both said they would be straight in. Somehow I made my way back to the ward and as I walked through the door a hush descended on the room: the women I had been laughing and joking with less than an hour ago now averted their eyes. I wanted to run as far away from the hospital as I could, but instead I sat on the bed and waited for my husband and mother to arrive. As soon as they arrived my composure went and with heavy hearts we paged the doctor. I was afraid to hear what the doctor had to say. As we were waiting for her to arrive, I repeated in my head, again and again, "I can cope with anything, God, please don't let Melody die. Please don't take her away from me."

The doctor began by saying that this was the worst part of her job and that unless she was a hundred per cent certain of her findings she would not put us through this. Gently she explained that our baby was seriously ill and its chances of surviving until birth were remote. Our baby was dying. As she spoke to us, the baby kicked and I remember telling her that she had obviously made a mistake. I asked her how could she tell me my baby was dying when I could feel the kicking. At the time I remember thinking how cruel she was being, taking away all hope. Now I know she was just preparing us for the inevitable.

As it happened, Glen's heart beat for the final time on New Year's Eve and I gave birth to him twelve days later.

Standing at Glen's grave that bitterly cold January day, with the echo of the song "Bright Eyes" ringing in my ears, I watched his tiny white coffin being lowered into the ground. I didn't think that I would ever be happy again. I could not imagine laughing again, or of living a day when my thoughts were not all of Glen.

However, the passage of time numbed that overwhelming grief and as each new day dawned, the awful pain slowly subsided. It took time, a lot of time. However, the day came when I woke up and my first thought was of something other than Glen.

The first time this happened to me, I felt a terrible sense of guilt. I felt that I had somehow betrayed Glen's memory. Then I pulled myself together and analysed how my mind was working. I realised that I didn't have to spend every minute of every day thinking about Glen to keep his memory alive. He would always live in my heart and nothing would ever take away the memory of him. He would always be a part of our lives and we would never forget him.

Through this experience, I realised that there was little literature available for people who were in my situation. During this time I had so many troubling questions in my head that I was too embarrassed to ask the doctors. Questions such as, "What does a dead baby look like?" or "Will I be afraid of my baby?" As it turned out, when my son was born I saw past what others didn't, and saw only my beautiful baby. I proceeded to write *If it Happens to You: Miscarriage & Stillbirth, A Human Insight*. It was the book I had needed, but which didn't exist. This was before the internet was the tool of learning and information it is today.

The book was widely read and put in maternity hospitals and libraries. Through the enormous feedback from the book, I realised that the power of the written word could make a difference. Not too long after my book was published, the Stillbirth Register, which I had assisted campaigning for, was introduced. At last babies who were stillborn after twenty-eight weeks' gestation were finally recognised. Two years and one day after Glen's birth, our daughter Sarah was born. She continues to bring us much joy today.

A year later I followed this book up with *You Have to Scream With Your Mouth Shut: Violence in the Home*, a book that represented some of the most silent victims in Irish society, victims of the heinous crime of domestic violence. It seemed for a period of time that every newspaper I read contained shocking stories of domestic violence. Although this issue didn't affect me personally, I began to question what happened to all the people whose stories weren't the focus of media attention; who suffered at the hands of an abuser in silence. I wanted to give a voice to those who would otherwise not be heard and to highlight their plight.

At the time of writing that book, I had two small children; lived in a small apartment as we were saving for a house; was working full-time and studying psychology at college. Additionally, my father dropped dead while talking to someone. Being determined to finish the book, I continued writing with the odds stacked against me and it was indeed a proud moment when the book hit the bestseller list during the week of its publication. I derived great satisfaction from the feedback to my books and I knew from talking to people and from letters I received that they had really made a difference to some people's lives.

The following years passed with the usual ups and downs of family life and raising children while pursuing a career. I worked variously as a journalist, editor, managing editor and then, in 2001, with the support of my family, I started my own publishing company. However, let me backtrack a little.

Finding out I only buried part of my son

In 1999 Alder Hey Children's Hospital in Liverpool hit the news. It transpired that the organs of deceased babies and children had been retained without the consent or knowledge of the parents. These weren't isolated cases. The scandal involved thousands of organs, many of which had been given to pharmaceutical companies. Donations had been made to some hospitals. The "cash for tissues" row quickly followed the scandal.

Parents were finding out that children, whom they thought they had buried whole, were often missing organs such as the brain, lungs, heart and abdominal organs. Many, who had been unaware they had buried their children with missing body parts, were forced to hold second and sometimes third funerals once the facts emerged and bodily organs were gradually returned. Others would never have this opportunity. It transpired that organ harvesting at Alder Hey had been such an established practice that even parents whose children had died decades earlier found that organs had been removed before the bodies were released to the families.

In December 1999, the British government announced it would be holding a public inquiry, following the revelations that other hospitals around Britain had also been retaining organs. Subsequently in 2001, Professor Liam Donaldson, the then Chief Medical Officer, told distressed parents that he would be backing a change in the law to ensure that hospitals could never again retain organs without permission. It seemed *The Human Tissue Act (1961)*, which made clear that doctors could not make a decision themselves on whether to keep organs unless the patient is a child who has died after a pregnancy lasting less than twenty-four weeks, did not prevent the organ harvesting of so many. However, new guidelines were introduced that would prevent this practice from ever happening again.

I remember when this news first broke I was absolutely appalled, and my heart went out to the parents who had been affected. I knew what it was like to bury a child and I could scarcely imagine how traumatic this must have been for them.

It was some months later, in the middle of writing an article about something completely unrelated, that a thought bolted through my mind. I don't know what put it there, but my blood ran cold and I could feel the hairs standing upright on my arms. The thought was so terrible to contemplate; so instead I tried to push it to the back of my mind.

I wrestled with my ensuing thoughts for quite a while, debating whether I would be better off not knowing what had happened. However, deep down I knew that, until I got the answer, I would not rest easy. Was this practice widespread in Irish hospitals? Had Glen's organs been retained without my consent? I had to know. A friend of mine, whose son died at birth as a result of the cord being wrapped around his neck, chose not to find out, and to this day, it is not something she ever wants to know.

My hand was trembling as I picked up the receiver to dial the number of the maternity hospital in which Glen was born. The receiver felt like a dead weight in my hand. It took quite a few attempts to pluck up enough courage to let the number ring. Although it rang only a couple of times before being answered, those seconds seemed like hours and my heart was beating so hard I could see it through my jumper. So many things were going through my head.

In time, my worst fears were confirmed; I had buried only the shell of my son. I quickly looked through the book I had written after he died, to see if there was anything in it that may not have seemed significant at the time, but now could be interpreted in a different way. I read through the pages with tears streaming down my face. My darling son had been taken asunder and never put back together again. It was almost too much to bear. I was so angry and so very sad. I had given my consent for an autopsy in the hope it would help other parents, but I had not given my consent for this.

There, on page 24, I silently read the words: ". . . *The doctor returned and asked me if I would sign a consent form* for a post-mortem to be done. She left it with me and said she would be back shortly. I sat there in a daze. One half of me was saying, 'He's gone through enough, let him rest in peace.' The other half was saying, 'If they can find anything that might help even one other baby, then his death will not have been in vain.' It took only a couple of minutes for me to decide that I should consent . . ."

I was almost afraid to read on, but I had to know if there were any clues, however innocuous they seemed at the time. Just three pages later, I got my answer. ". . . I had all the things I wanted to put into the coffin with me. As we went inside to the morgue, the doctor called Gerry aside and explained that the coffin had been closed and it would be best to leave it this way. He said that if Gerry really wanted him to open it then he would, but felt that it wouldn't be a good idea. The doctor assured us that he would personally put the things we had brought for Glen into the coffin himself. He told us that my mother had been there earlier with the clothes for Glen; the coffin had already been closed, but he had opened it and dressed Glen in the clothes my mother had brought . . ."

I put the book down and didn't know what to think. My worst fears had been confirmed; but was this the reason the coffin had been closed? It was something I would never really know for sure, but now believed the reason for this may not have been because of how he looked. It was almost ten years since I had buried him, and now, the pain and the raw emotion of his death were flooding back. Worse still, this trauma was compounded by having to deal with feelings of anger and revulsion at what had happened, and, of course, sadness. I felt that, as a mother, I had somehow failed my son by letting this happen to him. I promised him, there and then, that whatever it took, I would get answers and I would find out how such a thing had been allowed to happen. Someone had to be held accountable.

Some time later I went to the hospital and faced the pathologist who had removed Glen's organs. It was horrible being back in the hospital – the smells, the sounds and so many memories. A line from a song my husband had written for Glen kept going around and around in my head as we walked through the hospital: *"Passed an Entrance sign above an Exit door, our baby's coming home no more."* The meeting took place in an office, where I sat and listened to the pathologist talk, knowing that whatever he said would not change things, but perhaps it would answer my questions. I had to know what had been taken from my baby without my knowledge. I found out some of what I needed to know, which was the only reason I had attended the meeting.

I brought the meeting to an abrupt end after he uttered the words, "I know how you must feel." I couldn't believe my ears. This man, who had taken my son apart, was sitting there telling me he knew how I felt. It gave audacity new meaning and I looked straight at him, making sure I made eye contact, as I posed my final question, the words of which will always be etched on my brain. "Really?" I said quietly, "How many of your own children have you butchered?" With that I got up and left the room. I had to get out of the hospital and away from him as quickly as possibly, declining the offer to have a cup of coffee with a social worker, who had sat in on the meeting. I had made a silent promise to Glen on the way to the meeting that I would remain composed and dignified and I was glad I had kept my promise to him. I wanted him to have the dignity that had been cruelly taken from him in death; I wanted him to know that I would fight, on his behalf, for as long as it took. I had given him immortality by writing a book about him; now I wanted to give him justice. As soon as my husband and I got to our car, my composure shattered and I sobbed bitterly.

I felt no sense of closure even though I had some, but by no means all, of the answers. His organs had been incinerated the year previously, just like clinical waste, without anyone informing me. I had buried only part of my son, and the opportunity to bury his organs with him had been cruelly stolen from me. I struggled to come to terms with what had happened. This was unbelievable, like a horror film.

I met with Parents for Justice in 2000, a group set up by affected parents to campaign for answers and provide support to others who had been affected. However, at that time I wasn't ready to write a book. It was still too raw, too shocking and my anger was far too great to be able to write in any way objectively.

In a shocking development early in 2008, Parents for Justice was forced to vacate the offices from which they manned their helpline and dealt with thousands of enquiries every year, because what little funding they received was withdrawn. Furthermore, in March 2008, it was revealed that sand had been placed in the bodies of dead children to make up the weight of their missing organs.

A dream begins

In 2001 I started my own publishing company. With over a decade's experience in senior editorial positions, writing for the national press and with two books under my belt, it seemed like a natural progression. I didn't think twice about borrowing money, such was my conviction that things would work out.

Starting my own company permitted me to do something I loved. It allowed me to do what I do best – write. The magazines I produced were never going to make me rich, but they were platforms for issues that mattered to people. During the years I ran my company, I covered, among other things: gambling; domestic violence; homelessness; alcoholism; bullying; AIDS; child exploitation; debt; child abuse; and a whole array of other social and health issues.

As the company grew and the number of magazines I published increased, my eighteen-hour days were still not enough. In addition to running the company on a day-to-day basis, managing staff and attending meetings, I also wrote all the magazines on my own at night and it was hard work. There were often times when I worked three days straight, going home only to shower and change my clothes. Looking back, my company functioned to the exclusion of any personal life. Over the years there were cancelled family holidays, fragmented family life and a wife and mother who worked around the clock.

My passion for my company and, perhaps most importantly, my passion for my belief that I could somehow make it work, given the financial dire straits, meant I continued against the odds when retrospectively I should have stopped. Call it naivety, call it what you will, but I fought so hard to keep afloat, stopping was not an option for me.

When the company needed money – as it did, time and time again – I took out personal loans to ensure it continued trading. When I couldn't take out any more bank loans, I borrowed from friends, from family and even from children's savings. The stress of trying to do everything single-handedly, against ever-increasing odds, began to take its toll on my health. In the space of less than two years I was hospitalised four times and underwent surgery twice in three months.

My home burns down

Amid this, in the early hours of 22 July 2005, I experienced everyone's worst nightmare – a house fire. Up until that moment, to me, a house fire was something dreadful that only happened to "other" people.

I have always had a fear of fire. Like most people, we had fire blankets and fire extinguishers in the kitchen next to the cooker, and always checked that things were out and off around the house before going to bed at night. I had been working late and when my daughter came down from bed after waking, we chatted for a while before going upstairs. In fact, we were still chatting at 3.25 a.m. when there was a bang above us and one of my lights went out. As my son's bedroom was above, I assumed he had fallen out of bed (at the time my son was a strapping six-foot-two-inch eighteen-year-old), so the bang was loud enough for me to think this. As I ascended the stairs to his room I noticed a flickering. My first thought was that he had left the television on. However, before I reached the top, I realised that the glow was orange. By the time I reached him, the foot of his bed was on fire.

Amazingly, or not too amazingly for those of you with children of a similar age, he had slept through it. I woke him and we made one vain attempt to put the fire out. However, it was futile and, within seconds, I knew that if we were to get out alive we had no choice but to flee. As we left his room, a sheet of fire covered his bed. Every second counted as the fire started to spread. The speed at which it took hold is something only those who have been in this situation will really comprehend.

Unlike what I had only seen in movies up to this point, there was surprisingly little smoke. Just flame. After waking my husband, I went last down the stairs knowing that my home and everything in it was going to go up in flames before my eyes and there was nothing I could do to stop it. I dialled 999 as we were leaving the house.

My daughter's screams outside woke neighbours, who were beside us in minutes with clothes and blankets. Our immediate neighbours stood with us not knowing if the fire brigade would reach us before the fire spread to their house. I cannot adequately describe in words what it felt like to stand in front of my home and watch flames shooting through the roof. It was surreal; just minutes earlier I had been preparing to go to bed.

I watched, knowing that a lifetime of memories was being taken away from me. Glen's identity bracelet, his footprints and his handprints. Karl and Sarah's first shoes, first teeth, first pictures, first copybooks from school. The manuscript for my first book and the typewriter I used. Cards from loved ones like my grandfather, my grandmother and my father who were dead. And photographs, oh, so many photographs, books and magazine collections. These were the things I thought of; the things I knew could never be replaced.

The forensic investigator, Norman, who was there to assess what started the fire, came back to the house after he finished his examination, with floodlights and generators and, on his own time, helped us to search through charred debris for anything we could salvage. I will be eternally grateful to him for this. The pungent smell of smoke permeated the air and penetrated our clothes. For weeks after the fire, I could not banish the smell, even when I was nowhere near the house.

I remember the day of the fire, standing in the kitchen of my destroyed home, trying to organise rented accommodation, while at the same time continuing to sort problems at the office. I was in the middle of a big project for a client, and after the initial call of sympathy, the following day they sent work for me to take a look at. My daughter was going to summer camp the day after the fire and we had had her case packed. Now she only had the clothes she stood in. Between friends and family, we managed to organise clothes and toiletries in time for her to go away. I was insistent that she went, because I felt she was better away from the trauma. I knew that by the time she returned a week later, somehow we would have settled into rented accommodation.

The fire happened less than eight weeks after we had finally got rid of the builders who had been building an extension onto our house. While everything had been upside down, we had taken the opportunity to redecorate the house completely from top to bottom, put in wooden flooring and new wooden doors. There was a lot of stuff that had been destroyed in the fire that was literally only weeks old. The devastation was severe and ran well into six figures. It took six months for the house to be rebuilt, during which time we lived in a rented house just around the corner.

I hated the rented house – not because it wasn't a nice house, it was, but because it wasn't home. I was trying to work surrounded by boxes on a computer I wasn't used to, which was perched on a kitchen table, when I was used to working in my purpose-built office at home. For months after the fire I would go to get things, forgetting they had been destroyed in the fire. I remember trying to select tiles and wooden flooring and the like for the house with the builders in between meetings, not really giving a damn what they looked like, once they got the job done. I just wanted to go home.

The only thing I concerned myself with was the wiring and additional safety features I was having installed at the time of rebuilding. I don't know how many sockets there are in my house but, to give you an idea, there are twenty plug sockets in my kitchen and also twenty in my office. All have individual on/off switches and there are far more than we are ever likely to use, eliminating the need to ever have to use an extension lead or a three-way plug. Every room in the house is now linked to a central fire-alarm system.

I know insurance companies get bad press, and sometimes rightly so, but the man from my insurance company, Andy, was absolutely fantastic and to this day, we keep in touch. Although we were fully insured, no amount of contents cover will ever replace everything that has been lost and, of course, even if somehow it did, there will be things that no amount of money can ever replace. Losing my home, my memories, and its contents was traumatic and is something my children are still affected by to this day. However, I think I was so used to dealing with crises, I didn't allow myself fully to take in what had happened.

Two surgeries and the death of a dream

Two months later, when I needed it least, my General Manager left the office one day and, of his own accord, never returned. The reasons for his departure shall remain private, out of courtesy to his family, but suffice to say his behaviour made a bad situation far worse, and made the chance of the company ever recovering from what was already a precarious situation impossible.

Five months after the fire I underwent surgery. Over forty tiny blister-like growths were removed from my face. It was thought the stress brought on by the fire had caused this to happen. It was painful and my face was bandaged. I didn't have the luxury of recovery and went straight to the office after surgery knowing I looked like something out of a horror movie.

I spent the next couple of months working twenty-hour days, running myself into the ground trying to figure out ways and solutions that would keep the company afloat. Out of desperation, I went to my printer with a view to forming a partnership. Although I owed him some money, I had paid him hundreds of thousands of euro in printing costs over the years. I showed him the books and he kept my accountant hanging for ages before saying no. However, when I couldn't print a magazine through lack of funds and had to let it go, he immediately took it on and published it himself.

When driving back to the office after a meeting with him and his father, I suddenly got a searing pain across my stomach. This was different to any pain I had ever known; it was crippling and made me double up, and I had to pull in and let it pass before I continued driving. The intensity of it took my breath away. It worsened as the hours passed and I was literally floored by every wave of pain. I knew I would have to go to the hospital as I was in absolute agony, so Gerry brought me. After tests at the hospital, it was decided

I would need an operation to remove my gallbladder. After giving me a shot of morphine to ease the pain, the doctor commented that I was young to be suffering with this. However, it transpired I had a bad infection and I had to wait a further ten days for the infection to clear. I was drip-fed most of the time and I was a physical wreck. I was also worried about not being in the office to deal with things. After the operation I had to spend a further two weeks recovering, and tried to work as best I could from bed.

I exhausted every conceivable option for my company during the next few months, and swallowed what little pride I had left many times. Eventually the time came when I had nowhere left to turn. In the end, there was little regard for loyalty and I felt terribly betrayed by people I had trusted. I quickly learned, when the chips are down, that there is no friendship in business.

I had always tried to do the right thing. In the most appalling personal circumstances, when it would have been so easy to walk away, I stayed and fought because I believed in a dream and because I had given everything I had to give to my company at the exclusion of a personal life. I had effectively missed six years of my children's lives, of cancelling holidays at the last minute, of living . . . and for what? Stopping was an agonising decision that ripped my heart out, for I knew I would never start again. This, I believe, was the final event that prompted the start of a meltdown that had been a very long time in the making.

The Year that was a Breakdown

"Every word is like an unnecessary stain on silence and nothingness."

SAMUEL BECKETT

November

Having exhausted every conceivable avenue, I made the agonising decision to go into liquidation. To be honest, by then I wasn't left with any choice. For a long time people had been advising me to stop. They saw what it was doing to me and rightly figured that nothing was worth that. I had worn myself out and didn't give up until circumstances absolutely backed me into a corner from which there was no way out. This was the first time that something had happened in the company that I couldn't fix, and the feeling of failure was something I hated. I felt as if nobody really knew what the implications of closing would be for me, not only on a financial front, but also on an emotional front. People reasoned that if I removed the stress, I would start feeling better. However, for me, it was simply a case of one type of stress being replaced with another and I was despairing.

The night before my fortieth birthday, I moved into an apartment. It was a sudden decision and it was the first time in my adult life that I had lived alone. It was a decision that caused my family much confusion and upset,

40

but at the time I really believed it was the right thing to do. It was probably the only time in my life that my instinct had proved me wrong and, in the process, I deeply hurt those I loved. It was six weeks before the company closed and part of me didn't want my family to bear witness to what was going to happen. I felt so overwhelmed by things and felt there was nobody I could talk to, who could really understand what I was going through.

I went back home the following morning because I knew the children would want to see me on my fortieth birthday. The look of confusion in their eyes and my husband's eyes was more than I could bear. What I was doing made complete sense to me, yet retrospectively, I hadn't a clue what I was doing . . . but thought I did. I was probably as far away as possible from where I had envisaged I would be at this point in my life. I thought life was supposed to begin at forty, but for me, life as I knew it had ended. Much of the month was taken up with meetings with my accountant and winding things down in advance of the liquidation meeting the following month.

December

With the final preparations made and final accounts complete, all that remained was to say goodbye to the last of my staff, who had stayed with me to the bitter end. As we walked out the door together for the last time, I found it hard to believe that this was actually happening. After our lunch I returned alone to the office. I spent some time walking around rooms that once bore so many hopes and dreams; then I went into my own office and got lost in thought. I put some personal things in a box and then left the building knowing I would never return.

The liquidation meeting was nerve-wracking. I stood before a room full of people, many of whom I once thought of as friends, and made my case. My knees were knocking together and my mouth was dry. It was as if this was happening to someone else; I couldn't believe that this was how my dream was ending. In the end, I had done everything humanly possible to continue, but the odds were far greater than I could deal with.

I walked out of that meeting knowing that life was never going to be the same. I had walked away from everything I had known and, in less than two years, had lost my home, my family, every penny I had, my business and my job. I was also in catastrophic debt from the collapse of the business. I was numb. I went straight to a pub and promptly got drunk. As Christmas revellers sang along to Christmas songs in the pub, I wondered what on earth I was going to do.

That Christmas was unlike any Christmas I had ever known. It was heartbreaking not to have been there when the children woke and opened their presents; I wondered how they had felt without me there. I drove over to the house to collect them and bring them over to my apartment, where I had tried to replicate the Christmas traditions we had always had. It was a completely surreal experience. As I sat outside waiting for them, I looked at the house that I knew would always be my home. I couldn't go in; it was far too painful. I knew I could go back at any time, and I felt so bad about everything that had happened. The children and my mother left late that afternoon to return home from their dinner with Gerry and I felt an overwhelming sense of sadness and of failure. I felt worthless and that the only thing I was any good at was hurting people, in particular those I loved most.

I spent that New Year's Eve in the UK, primarily with a group of people I didn't know. As Big Ben chimed in the New Year, I stood alone outside, as the champagne corks popped and everyone sang "Auld Lang Syne". I knew this was going to be a very difficult moment for me and I didn't want to break down in front of strangers. This was the first time in my entire life that I had not been with my mother on New Year's Eve, the first time in twenty-two years I had not been with Gerry, and the first time in my children's lives that I had not been with them.

When I rang home they told me there were no celebrations; that it just wasn't the same without me there. My heart was breaking. Celebrating was the last thing on my mind as I returned indoors. I remember phoning a friend later that night sobbing inconsolably and saying that I wanted to get on a flight home. The fact that it was three in the morning on New Year's Day didn't enter my head; I just wanted to go home.

January

I had no job to return to after the Christmas break and for the first time, for as long as I could remember, I actually had nothing to do and I hated it. For years, when I had no time to do anything, I had dreamed about doing nothing, but now that this was the case, I couldn't stand it. I was able to immerse myself in work and not have time to think. Now, this great expanse of time stretched out in front of me and I had nothing to fill it with, except thoughts. For the first time in well over a decade I had stopped, and memories of all the things that had happened to me before and during this time began to flood my mind. These were the thoughts I had pushed to the recesses of my mind and now they consumed my every thought. I couldn't get away from them or stop them.

I was thinking about writing a book (not this one), but try as I did, I just couldn't apply my mind to it. My concentration was minimal; I wasn't aware then that depression attacks your cognitive senses and rational thought. I knew that it was only a matter of time before the financial fallout from the business began and I wasn't altogether sure how I was going to deal with that. I was still paying my share of all the bills at home in addition to those I was incurring with the apartment, on a fraction of the income I was used to. Then there were all the credit cards that I amassed over the years. Making repayments had never posed a problem, until now. I applied for jobs I was over-qualified for, but without success. I was consulting, but it wasn't enough to cover the multitude of bills and loan repayments.

In the middle of that month, the liquidator repossessed my car because it had been a company car. I had lost everything else and now what little independence I had left was being taken. Although it was financially crippling, I hired a car at the expense of other things. Nothing was going to stop me seeing my children. I had continued to go up to the house every morning after I left to collect my daughter and bring her to school. It was the last bit of normality in my increasingly abnormal and irrational world.

My bowel was acting up terribly and although it appeared to be related to irritable bowel syndrome, there was a question mark because it was so severe. Even the smallest meal was resulting in my making a mad dash to the loo. I was finding it exhausting, restrictive and very painful. My doctor made an appointment with a specialist to see if he could establish what was wrong.

I attended a mediation meeting with my husband. It was the first time I had seen him since leaving and I had been dreading it. He was as lovely as ever and asked how I was feeling, but the dark circles under his eyes showed he was not finding things easy either. It was a strange situation for both of us; we had battled so much as a team; now we were battling the same thing, but separately. The meeting was awful, and I left before it was due to finish because I found it so upsetting. This situation was unlike most; I felt totally responsible, so there were none of the usual issues people attending mediation generally present with.

The rest of that month passed in much the same way; I would spend every day worrying and go to bed every night without thinking of a solution. I started to feel despondent about things and it started to become an effort to do anything. I was exceptionally irritable and frustrated and felt very alone.

February

The feeling of isolation grows. Having been so used to working eighteen-hour days, I found it hard to adapt to doing nothing. I quickly realised that there were worse things in life than being needed. Not being needed was devastating. Bills started to pile up and, rather than confront the problem, I put them unopened into a desk drawer. When the drawer was full, I started using a large box. At first I didn't want to open them because I was frightened of what they may say. However, as my depression deepened I didn't have the energy to open them, even had I wanted to. My computer remained virtually untouched; I just didn't have the will or the concentration to write. I was finding it harder and harder to apply myself to anything. It was as if my interest in everything had been taken away.

My sister came with me on the day of my surgery and waited until I was taken to theatre. At the back of my mind were a million "what-ifs". This was probably the first and only time that I ever let the thought enter my head that stress could be to blame – probably because, with nothing to hide behind, I was aware of the ever-increasing level of stress I was under. The results of the surgery were inconclusive and I was advised to wait a while and then book in for further tests. In the meantime, all I could do was learn to live with it.

I noticed myself starting to withdraw socially. Where I used to go out with friends regularly, now I found myself looking for excuses not to. I did make an attempt once to explain how I was feeling to someone, but they couldn't empathise with what I was going through or how I was feeling, which made me feel stupid and much worse than I already felt. It was possibly the first time in my life I really opened up and allowed myself to be vulnerable. I was never good at opening up; I'm still not, and it had taken quite a lot for me to do it. After this, I put my shutters up and would not speak to anyone about what was happening. I felt alone, so very, very alone. Writing this now, I can place myself back during this time and can recall, with absolute clarity, my feelings during this time.

March

My sense of despair was increasing and I was really starting to struggle financially. Things were starting to overwhelm me and I felt like I was looking at life through a fog. Trying to maintain two homes was quickly swallowing up what little money I had left, and my existence became meagre – not easy when you associate with people who don't have money worries. Pride stopped me from telling anyone how bad it really was. I became even more reclusive and by now, I went around with a constant knot in my stomach worrying about bills, about creditors and about how I was going to survive.

The bills continued to pile up and, in what was my last act of trying to control my situation, I sat down and wrote to every company outlining my situation, asking them, under the exceptional circumstances, to make allowances. However, I never knew what they said because I couldn't open their replies. Many weeks later, my sister saw the gravity of the situation and the amount of unopened post, picked up her phone and, on my behalf, sought help to deal with my finances. Part of me was so relieved that somebody had taken control, but I was slowly reaching the point of not caring. I knew that when I reached it, I would also have reached the point of no return. The dynamics of keeping it together would be irrevocably damaged. I used to lie in bed at night trying to think. I was finding it hard to assemble thoughts cohesively and wondered if how I was feeling was normal. I desperately wanted someone to understand; to tell me it was going to be okay, but instead I hid my terror and struggled on, too embarrassed to tell anyone or ask for help.

April
The feeling of despondency overwhelmed me and one morning I couldn't muster the energy or inclination to get out of bed. I remember thinking that I had absolutely no reason to get up most of the time; so, I reasoned, why bother making the effort? Up until then I had forced myself to get up and dressed every day in an effort to maintain some kind of normal routine. Although I didn't realise it then, my depression had taken a turn for the worse. I began using sleeping tablets to sleep my way through days and, on one occasion, my sister threatened to break the door down if I didn't get up and let her in. I

found it a huge effort to talk to people and the thought of going out socially filled me with dread. I just wanted to be left alone to lie in bed; I felt such a failure and I felt utterly useless. I was also very angry with myself for not being able to cope. Oh, how the mighty have fallen, I frequently thought to myself. I became a virtual recluse. It felt as if the walls of the apartment were closing in on me and my solution was to stay in bed and not get up.

I knew switching off and not communicating was driving my family to distraction. It wasn't that I didn't want to; it was that I couldn't. I was emotionally shattered; my concentration, logic, memory, reasoning and interpretation no longer worked. I saw the situation as catastrophic and although it was pretty serious, my ability to think in any way positively had been distorted and eroded by depression.

I made one further effort at compiling a job application. This was a mammoth undertaking. What should have taken an hour or so to put together took three very long days and totally drained me. The simple act of putting sentences together totally overwhelmed me. As someone who writes for a living, this had a profound impact on me. I finally completed it, emailed it and promptly returned to bed.

I look back now and wonder how, as a person who always has to be doing something, I lay in bed for so long doing nothing? I couldn't concentrate long enough to read or to follow a television programme properly. Hours would pass without me moving; I was somehow lost in time and living in a world where it made no difference to me whether it was day or night, a weekday or the weekend. I had no idea of what was going on around me, and although I found what was happening to me very frightening, I was absolutely powerless to do anything about it.

One of the very few times I ventured out that month was to attend the meeting my sister had arranged with Money Advice Budgeting Services (MABS). I didn't want to go to it, primarily because I didn't want to go out, but there was also a feeling a shame and humiliation at having to avail of their services. I had written about this organisation many times over the years, always in a positive light and always giving it great credit for the work it did. Now, here I was, using it myself. The MABS office was a short stroll from Dundrum Town Centre, so I decided to park there and walk down. I wasn't prepared for what happened as I walked through the centre. All of a sudden I was filled with terror. My heart was racing, I found it difficult to breathe, I felt as if I were going to faint and knew that I had to get out of the centre. It was the longest walk of my life. As soon as I made it outside, I sat on a wall, not knowing what was happening. Was I dying? Was I going mad? Was I having a heart attack? After a few minutes, my heart stopped racing and I felt my body relax. I realised that I had had a panic attack and it was not a pleasant thing. Often the physical symptoms of depression are forgotten.

I made my way to the MABS office, not really knowing what to expect. I passed by it at first and had to ring to find out its exact location. It was tucked away at the end of a quiet lane and was very welcoming. Ruth, the woman my sister had spoken with on my behalf, met me in reception. We went into an office and I felt comfortable with her from the moment we met. She exuded a feeling of calmness and she didn't bat an eye as I emptied the huge pile of unopened letters onto the desk. She made me feel as if this was perfectly normal and I knew that I could trust her and that she wasn't there to sit in judgement of me. I will never be able to articulate the help and support Ruth gave me and, indeed, continues to give me. She never appeared daunted by what she saw or by what I told her, though I strongly suspect that my personal debt was one of the largest she had ever come across.

The first thing she did was to reassure me. Debt was a labyrinth she had navigated many times. She immediately set about writing to my creditors again in an effort to stave off any impending action they might take. She then told me she would sort through the mound of bills and get an accurate figure for my debt. I remember walking out of her office that day, asking myself why I hadn't sought help sooner. I knew the answer, of course. It was one less thing to worry about in the immediate future, but I knew it was only a matter of time before I found out just how much debt I was really in.

I remember walking into my doctor's surgery one day and telling him that I was having a breakdown. Having seen me go through so many traumas and bounce back, I don't think at first he really understood the enormity of what I was telling him. I wasn't going to bounce back this time. In fact, I felt like I was freefalling into an abyss so deep it would quickly swallow me. He prescribed anti-depressants but, knowing me as well as he did, he didn't suggest counselling. I think he knew I would not have benefited from this particular method of treatment, particularly at this time. I left with a prescription in my hand, not really knowing if they were going to make a difference. I experienced no side effects after starting these, though I had discussed the possibility with my doctor.

May

This month my son moved into the apartment with me. I had two bedrooms, but one was Sarah's for when she stayed with me. Karl alternated between sleeping in this room when Sarah wasn't there and sleeping on the sofa. However, even though it was great to have them with me, they could not loosen the grip depression had on me. Ruth contacted me later in the month to tell me that my personal debt was well over six figures and it deeply shocked me. I knew it was a lot, but I hadn't banked on it being this much. All this debt and I hadn't a single thing to show for it. I felt as if someone had pulled the ground from under me. I was already struggling and I felt myself absolutely despairing.

June

Out of the blue I got a call to say the contract for my consultancy was being terminated without notice. To say that this was a shock doesn't begin to cover how I felt. There was a lot of business history between myself and the person I had the contract with and it was always a concern that one day something like this would happen. However, a verbal assurance by him to a board of people and a written contract assuaged my fears somewhat. He said the work I was doing could be done in-house saving him money. I could invoke a three-month notice clause, but this didn't solve my problems, which, in an instant, had increased tenfold.

I could feel my head getting light. I felt so betrayed and stupid. On entering into the contract, my gut instinct had told me it wasn't going to be a happy union. I had got the position on foot of arranging a contract between him and former clients of mine and a condition of the deal was that I was given a consultancy position. It took days for the enormity of what happened to sink in and I could feel myself getting more and more apathetic. Although I informed my former clients about the situation, I quickly learned that, in business, there is no such thing as friendship. It was a truly bitter lesson to learn.

Gerry came over to the apartment and we had a long chat about things. We discussed all that had happened, how I was feeling, and the possibility of me going home. So much had happened, yet, in many ways, it was as if nothing had happened. We talked about it many times subsequently, but with my fuzzy way of thinking, I put it to the back of my mind.

July

I felt as if my mind was made of cotton wool. I could no longer think properly and I could not see a future. I had an overwhelming urge to run until I could run no more – far, far away. Not forever, but at that moment I doubted my purpose in life, my ability as a mother and my worth

53

as a person. I was asked to attend an interview for the position I had applied for in April. It was the last thing I felt like doing, but I attended because deep down I knew that if I didn't make one last effort to try and escape from the clutches of depression, it was going to drag me under. The interview went extremely well and I was confident I would get the position. I was later offered the position, but it wasn't vacant for seven weeks.

I borrowed money from Gerry to go away to the UK for a few days and he brought me to the airport and collected me when I got back. I was completely distracted and wandered aimlessly around the airport, completely oblivious to my surroundings. I missed my flight, but managed to book another. I came back again two days later, but within hours decided to return to the UK. I didn't know what I wanted to do; I didn't want to be in the apartment and I didn't want not to be in the apartment; my mind wouldn't tell me what to do. I returned to the UK the following morning, armed with enough sleeping pills to sleep around the clock if I wanted to. I stayed for three days and came back more confused than I was when I arrived, with my confidence of my perception of things in tatters.

The medication I was on was making little difference so the doctor increased my dosage. I spent increasing amounts of time in bed and I had reached a point where I no longer wanted to exist. This is not to be confused with the desire to kill myself, for I never contemplated this. I just wanted the turmoil to stop. The how and why were things I gave no thought to.

August

I started the job I had attended the interview for in April at the end of the month. I took it in the hope that it would snap me out of the depression I was in. I would be forced to think about something other than my problems for eight hours a day, but they were never far away. My limbs felt like wood and I was permanently tired, but I struggled on. I got a letter from the landlord asking me to vacate the apartment when the lease expired the following month. She was finding commuting too much and wanted to move back to Dublin. It was a blow and the last thing I needed. The thought of having to move everything was overwhelming, so I pushed it to the back of my mind and pretended it had never happened. It was the only way I could deal with it. Much of my stuff was still in boxes in the apartment, as I had never unpacked it. When I moved in, I didn't know where home would eventually be, but I knew it would never be here.

September

As I held a responsible position and was writing for a national Sunday newspaper, I had to keep my head together as best I could. I was finding it increasingly difficult to function, but made sure my work was flawless. I had lost my pride many times by now, but I was determined not to lose pride in what I wrote. I would set my alarm clock for two hours before I had to get up, because that was how long it took me to psych myself up enough to get out of the bed. I would come back from work and go straight to bed on the nights my daughter wasn't staying with me. I no longer went out with friends and lived for the weekends when I didn't have to get out of bed at all. On Sunday evenings it would take me hours to select my outfits in advance for the following week, for doing it on a daily basis would have completely overwhelmed me. I briefly thought about going to my employer and explaining the situation, but after being there a while, I knew this wasn't going to be an option. I believe that, had I felt I could do this, and with their support, I may have been able to work through the depression a little better, because I liked the job. However, depression teaches you to be a master of disguise and a mistress of illusion. It was getting ever more difficult to keep up this façade and I knew that I was too sick to continue it. It was a horrible feeling and I was so angry with myself, but I was tired – very, very, tired.

I worked on a freelance basis from the apartment for a while, but even this got too overwhelming for me and eventually fell by the wayside some weeks later. I was now at my lowest point, without income from any source, too sick to work and facing the prospect of having to move. I wanted not to feel anymore.

THE FINAL MELTDOWN

"The darkest hour has only sixty minutes."

MORRIS MANDEL

October

The clock was ticking on the apartment front. My mother gave me money to cover living expenses and I will always be grateful for her support, emotional and financial, during my illness. With a sense of complete apathy I took the first apartment I saw advertised that was close to home. I have only traumatic memories of my time in this apartment, which were some of the worst months in my life. Retrospectively it was a very bad decision. The apartment complex overlooked my local shops – the shops I had been using since moving into my home well over a decade earlier. It was the strangest feeling to be living opposite them. My daughter said that I was so close to home I should come home, and she was right, although I didn't see this at the time. Throughout I had made a Trojan effort to continue leaving my daughter to school daily and it impacted me very negatively when I could no longer do this.

I would lie in bed listening to the sounds of everyday life outside and wonder if I would ever be part of it again. I began to depend more and more on tablets to function and stopped going out altogether. My mother brought my daughter to school every day and Gerry would often get off work early to collect her. I was in such a state, my daughter never stayed one night in that apartment during the two months I was there. In a complete reversal of roles, my son assumed the responsibility of looking after me. He made sure there was food in the fridge and that I had water. I hated what I had become, but I was too tired mentally, physically and emotionally, to do anything about it.

How I wanted to feel nothing. I took sleeping tablets around the clock to numb my brain, and during periods of lucidity would write articles for the paper. It was getting more difficult to function and I began to live in a permanent haze. My son used to get back from work, not knowing what state to expect me to be in. On a good day I would be awake and talk to him, albeit the conversation, like my attention span, was limited.

Ruth had managed to stave off my creditors up to this time, but they were starting to demand payment. I had nothing to give and all she could do was tell them this. At this juncture, I feel compelled to say that Ruth has worked so many miracles and I will always be grateful to her for her professional and compassionate manner when dealing with me. Again, my family all asked me to consider going home, but I couldn't. It would be the final admission that I could not cope, which was entirely correct, but I refused to see it this way. I wanted to tell someone about the despair I was feeling, but shame stopped me from talking, even to my family.

Gerry helped me move to the new apartment. He unpacked most of my stuff and set up my computer and other bits and pieces for me, aware of my worsening condition. He again asked me to come home, but I couldn't, so instead he just made sure he was around to keep an eye on me. I subsequently found out that my son had been liaising with him and my mother and sister for many months. Gerry popped in almost daily during my time in the apartment with food, newspapers and to make sure I had clean bed linen and towels. He assumed the responsibility like a worried parent; making sure I had enough to eat and drink, would take washing home and bring it back freshly laundered, would insist on my getting out of the bed so he could change the bedclothes. We had another long conversation about me going back and about us returning to normal. Both of us knew that twenty-two years counted for something; we were, after all, each other's best friend and loved each other.

November

In November I felt decidedly worse. Although apathetic, it was not enough to drown the feeling of despair. Nothing really mattered anymore, but paradoxically, I still worried myself sick about my debt and its consequences. I became totally reclusive, and could no longer muster the energy to get out of bed. Although I analysed my behaviour constantly and correctly diagnosed what was wrong, I was powerless to do anything about it. I'd take sleeping tablets then fight sleep to lie awake watching Sky News repeat itself throughout the night. I lacked the concentration needed to read, which, as a voracious reader normally, was devastating. I had no medium in which to escape.

I ventured out of the apartment to go back home for a birthday tea with my family. Gerry collected me from the apartment and also left me back. Everything was still the same and it was reassuring and heart-wrenching in equal measures. I didn't know it then, but I was only weeks away from returning.

I slept my way around the clock in an effort to blot out life. I kept the curtains closed and I existed in a state of semi-darkness around the clock. I didn't want to be awake – but I didn't want to be dead either – I just wanted not to feel anything. Gerry and the rest of my family's concern intensified and, for the first time, they were desperately worried that I would accidentally harm myself.

I started rebelling against the tablets I had been prescribed. I became ambivalent and battled with taking the tablets and the consequences of not taking the tablets. I felt as if I should be able to sort my problems without being pumped full of chemicals, which controlled how I acted, how I slept, how I existed. I started to deeply resent my medication and despised myself for needing it.

I started to go for late night strolls on my own. I would take my sleeping medication, then get dressed, not caring what I wore, and go out walking. I was numb to the point that I could convince myself nothing was wrong. I was oblivious to anything around me and, on a couple of occasions, got lost finding my way back to the apartment. Other times I'd get back to find the door of the apartment wide open because I had forgotten to close it on my way out. There were times I rang Gerry because I had locked myself out, only for him to come straight down and find the keys in whatever bag I had with me. To this day, I am still too embarrassed to go back to some of the shops I went into on these strolls. I did nothing terrible, but I know I must have looked wretched.

At the end of that month Gerry and Karl insisted on taking me to hospital, fearing that I had accidentally overdosed. I had not, for even in my darkest days, I was very careful with the medication I took. I was livid not only that they had done this, but also that they had involved strangers in the process. Retrospectively, I was very grateful to both of them. I remember waiting to see the doctor with them and being very indignant. I wouldn't sit with them and spoke only through gritted teeth to them.

When the doctor arrived I rattled off all my rights as a patient and, in particular, my right to patient confidentiality, which I promptly invoked. I left him with no choice but to ask Gerry and Karl to leave the room. He was a nice man, but no match for my annoyance at the situation, combined with my knowledge of both health legislation and law (which I had also studied). Although it wasn't a requisite to being discharged, to pacify my family I spoke to a psychiatrist before leaving. After briefly establishing the situation, insofar as what I elected to tell him, we spent much of that meeting discussing issues other than my health. Looking back, it would have been an ideal opportunity to unburden myself, but shame stopped me.

I remember him walking back with me to Gerry and Karl, who were waiting. He knew I wasn't suicidal, because I had told him that if I were suicidal, I certainly would not fail and I certainly would not be standing talking to him. I am sure he knew I was severely depressed, but I am equally sure he knew by me that I had no intention of taking my own life. My family were astonished that I left the hospital that night with a prescription for the very tablets I had not only been abusing, but hours earlier had presented with suspected of overdosing on. My faith in medical intervention and support was non-existent as I walked out. This was something that was further reinforced by a doctor I saw shortly afterwards and by the one counsellor I did see (albeit very briefly).

My own GP was away, so I agreed to go with Gerry to see a different doctor a few days later, who had been recommended. He changed the medication I had been on for many months and, as a result, I began to feel quite woozy all the time. I hated the semi-state of consciousness it had me in. However, the only thing I really cared about was having enough tablets to sleep. Looking back, he saw me in a given state, at a given time, and had no clue about the history or indeed the person I really was.

December

During my waking hours I was going around in a permanent daze. I was irrational and irritable. Things that made no sense to others, made utter sense to me. My son and his girlfriend saw me during these darkest days and frequently had to make sure that I was safely in bed before they went out. More often than not, they stayed in to "baby-sit".

I slept my way through the early weeks of December. I did venture out to buy Christmas presents, but ended up either buying things many times, forgetting I had previously bought them, and also buying things, that, at the time, I just *had* to have. Many months later I was still finding some of these purchases. I remember coming across plug-in timers for fan heaters in a bag; the fact that I had central heating was totally irrelevant when I bought not one, but five of them.

The dates for a trip to Copenhagen with my friend, which had been booked much earlier in the year, came and went. I slept through the days leading up to it and also during the time we were supposed to be away. My friend, bless her, didn't remark on it. I only realised it many weeks later of my own accord. I felt terribly embarrassed, but knew she wouldn't hold it against me. She knew there was nothing to be gained by giving out to me and instead simply booked another trip for three months down the line. These are the kind of friends you need; ones who don't judge, don't lecture and, most importantly, don't give up on you.

Unknown to me, Gerry and the rest of my family were discussing the situation and the best plan of action to take. Shortly before Christmas they decided that I should return home. As I remained in bed all the time, Gerry and Karl packed up all my things without me noticing and took them to the house. By the time I noticed what had happened, all that remained was the contents of my bedroom. Gerry contacted the landlord and arranged to discharge my lease. By now, I was too weak to fight and allowed myself to be brought home without resistance. Shame still prevented me from talking.

Everyone was delighted to have me home and I felt as if I were finally safe and back where I belonged. Although

I spent most of that Christmas period in bed, I came downstairs on Christmas morning to watch the kids open the presents that I had struggled so hard to wrap the night before. I was daunted by the task, but I was determined to do it and declined all Gerry's offers of help. I remained in my pyjamas, but came down again for Christmas dinner. My mother had come to stay over Christmas, as she had done since my father died, and for the first time in over a year, our family was finally back together again.

In a strange way, I knew that I had been silently screaming for help for a long time and I was more at peace than I had been in a very long time. Gerry and the kids were brilliant, bringing me meals in bed, sitting on the bed talking to me – but never pushing and not once, ever, voicing blame about my actions.

Slowly I began to see a glimmer of light, but knew I still had some way to go. I spent a lot of time in bed, with boxes everywhere because I was simply too overwhelmed to unpack them. However, I had started to read again, to think again, and to feel again. At one minute past midnight on New Year's Day, sitting watching the New Year being brought in on television in my pyjamas with Gerry, I made the decision to get better; a decision I owed to him and to my family and their unwavering love. It was time to give something back, to start making amends. I decided to come off every tablet I was on. I have an all-or-nothing personality, so gradually reducing – like you are supposed to – simply didn't cross my mind.

THE ROAD TO RECOVERY

"Hope is tenacious. It goes on living and working when science has dealt it what should be its death blow."

PAUL LAURENCE DUNBAR

I knew the bedroom looked like it had been ransacked; there were boxes stacked everywhere – some of which were half open, with their contents strewn on the floor. Every available surface was stacked high with various belongings. It proved difficult to navigate a path from the bed to the en-suite, so I learned how to step over and walk around the clutter. The chaos of the room resembled the chaos of a life; that I was tentatively – but determinedly – sorting out, working my way through, and slowly putting back together again. I got it into my head that this was something I had to do myself, so I politely declined all Gerry's offers of help to sort the boxes, which, retrospectively, as a very tidy person, must have been driving him mad.

I started feeling dizzy. It wasn't the kind of dizziness one feels getting up suddenly or stepping off an amusement ride. It was a dizziness that persisted all day, every day. My head was spinning and there was a constant buzzing in my ears, which drove me to distraction; I couldn't bear it. I quickly ascertained that it was withdrawal symptoms because I had stopped taking my anti-depressants suddenly *(you can read more about SSRIs in Chapter 2)*. As I was only just starting to see parts of the "old me" reintroduce themselves into my life, I didn't want anything to compromise this.

I made an appointment to see my doctor. That consultation was a very long one and I got some rather exasperated looks from those waiting, when I eventually emerged from his office. It was the first time I had spoken about my depression and, in so doing, I was admitting for the first time that I hadn't been able to solve the situation on my own, even though I thought I could. Although we both knew, sitting there, that he knew all about what had gone on, through my family and the hospital, I had never discussed it and had avoided seeing him through embarrassment. I knew at that minute that I was firmly on the road to recovery. I had found it so difficult to ask for help and, more than once, I thought of how difficult it must be for men to ask for help *(see male depression, Chapter 5)*.

That same day I saw a counsellor, but left after about fifteen minutes, because I had no faith in someone who gasped as I recounted some of the things that had happened to me. I needed someone who wasn't going to flinch at anything I said. I know I was probably just unlucky with this person, and I know that if I had searched I would have found someone more suitable, but combined with my dislike of talking, I chose to take it as a sign.

I still wasn't back to normal, but I was feeling better and stronger with each passing day. I started going out again. Not socially, but to the shops and back. It was a huge step on the road to recovery and I now looked to the future. I knew when I started putting nail varnish on and doing my hair that my recovery was well underway. I thought about all that happened constantly: I dissected, I analysed, I researched, I read and I reasoned. My brain was working once again and it was working overtime. I needed answers and wouldn't rest until I got them. I set up my computer in my office, which had lain there untouched since I got back. When the kids saw me doing this they looked delighted because it meant "mum" was coming back to herself and also to them.

Finding out about depression had given me back a sense of purpose. I wanted to understand everything there was to know about it. I wanted to see if the shame and embarrassment I felt was indicative of what most people felt or if I was an isolated case. I felt "alive" again and it was great. I found myself humming along to songs on the radio as I researched. I cannot tell you how good it was to start writing again. Nothing major, just putting thoughts onto paper, but the words tumbled out. I ran out of paper for my printer and, as I lived not too far away from a stationery shop, I decided to pop out and get some. A car-crash on the way meant I never made it.

As I say at the start of this chapter, I have little memory of the accident, probably as a result of hitting my head. I remembering driving to the shop and I remember a loud bang. To this day I still try to remember what happened but, so far, I have been unable to recall anything of the accident or of the following days.

I sustained various injuries, some of which took many weeks to heal. I was confined largely to bed, pumped full of various medications to relieve pain and reduce swelling, with no car and very restricted movement, and at that, on crutches. I couldn't believe that, just as things were starting to improve, fate had dealt me such a cruel blow. Although Gerry and the kids were brilliant and made me as comfortable as possible, I immediately relapsed. However, I quickly decided I did not want to return to the hellhole of severe depression, which to me was far worse than any of the injuries I sustained. I was annoyed at myself for being so weak, but rather than dwell on it, I resolved that it wouldn't happen again. Life was bound to throw things at me and I had to face them rather than run from them, as I had done before.

Friends of mine from Holland had been due to visit, but had to postpone due to my injuries. I was in no position to entertain people, which annoyed me. However, after a period of lying in bed and moping around, feeling sorry for myself, I decided that enough was enough and I got tough. I made a start, unpacking some of the boxes in my room, and made sure to get up early every day. I became adept at getting around on crutches and did exercises every day to strengthen my leg. I continued my research into depression and, at the insistence of a friend, made rough notes about my own experience. I again made a decision to come off the anti-depressants but this time I enlisted the help of my doctor who agreed to decrease the dose. We agreed that I would continue to take them, even though I was feeling better, both to prevent a recurrence and to reduce the likelihood of side effects. I must stress to anyone who is considering stopping their medication because they are feeling better to consult with their doctor before doing so *(see more about this in Chapter 2)*.

As I was confined to the house, I didn't worry too much about my appearance; my family were well used to the way I usually dressed when writing. I was absorbed in my writing and it mattered little whether I wrote in my pyjamas, a t-shirt and leggings or a black suit. The words came out regardless. I remember opening the door to my postman one morning. I had known him years, but the look of utter disbelief on his face (which he tried hard to conceal) when he saw me was absolutely comical and something I still smile at when I think of it. How I looked didn't cross my mind before I opened the door and spoke to him, just as I had done many times over the years . . . usually dressed in a business suit with perfect hair and perfect make-up. I didn't twig this until much later that morning when I happened to catch sight of myself in a mirror. I bore an uncanny resemblance to Einstein in the hair department and actually laughed out loud and, indeed, have since laughed with the postman about it!

In the following weeks I faced some testing times, but battled my way through them, refusing to get bogged down or stressed. I installed a new programme on my computer that had been sitting in its box for over year. However, the disk got caught in the drive and halted everything from working. I asked my mother to bring it to a repairman I had not used before. I reasoned that it was a simple job, and only I was afraid of doing damage, I would have attempted to remove the disk myself. When I eventually got the computer back, the disk had been removed, but the screen was completely obscured with white noise. I could not see it, much less work on it.

I emailed the repairman to explain what had happened. He said to return the computer and he would fix it. Gerry brought it back to him. After a week of constant telephone calls asking about the return of my computer, he explained that it would cost €600 to fix and additionally, now needed a new drive. I didn't know whether to laugh or cry. All that had been wrong was that a disk was caught in the drive. Gerry collected it before I sent a curt email asking him to put the computer back to the condition it had been in when given to him. He effectively told me to get lost. Rather than get stressed about it, I calmly took the matter to the Small Claims Court and they took on my case. It was a major headache, but I wasn't going to pay to repair something that hadn't been broken. I was very pleased with the way I had handled the matter and gave myself a pat on the back. It was hard to believe that months earlier I was unable to pick up a phone or talk to people. It was only a small thing, but it was another big step and it further boosted my belief that I was certainly getting back to myself.

I started writing proposals for two book ideas; one of them being this book. My head was crammed with thoughts and I knew that I was ready to start writing. In fact, I was driven by an intense need to write. I contacted Poolbeg Press and outlined my ideas to them, and a meeting was arranged. It had been a while since I'd written a book and I wondered briefly to myself if I still had what it took. Although I had been constantly writing articles since my last book, these were a long way from sitting down and writing in excess of 70,000 words, many of them about something deeply personal.

I also battled with the thought of making my private illness so very public, and of being put under a spotlight – where I would give people I knew, people my family knew, and indeed people I didn't know – almost voyeuristic access to my private world. I debated the pros and cons relentlessly but, deep down, I knew it was something I had to do. There were times during my depression when I felt so alone; felt as if I was the only person in the world to go through this; felt too embarrassed to talk about it; felt as if I was going mad. I knew that if I had read a book in which I could have recognised my own symptoms and had my questions answered, I would not have felt quite as bad as I had. Feeling guilty for not being able to "snap out of it" was, I thought during my illness, a reflection of failure on my part. Not being able to get out of bed, or go out with friends, or talk to people, was, I felt, a personal weakness. Now I knew it wasn't. Now I knew that depression was an illness that takes its victim deeper and deeper into a pit of despair, where they cannot imagine ever being able to claw their way out. I now knew that, at its worst, depression has the potential to manifest itself in a kind of emotional paralysis, so . . . I signed a contract for my books.

The trip my friend booked loomed and this time I didn't hesitate. While we were away, she confided that she hadn't known what to expect from me on the trip. However, she didn't care because she knew I needed the break and was prepared to put up with whatever mood I was in, dark or otherwise. I opened up to her about all I had gone through and the relief of finally talking about it with someone I knew, who wasn't going to judge me, was immense.

I felt I couldn't do this with my family because they had suffered enough and there was no one else I felt comfortable talking with about it. I advise any person who is depressed to talk to somebody they trust – it doesn't matter who it is, once you are comfortable. As you will read throughout this book, doctors are, by far, the first point of contact for a person who thinks they may be suffering from depression. While it is important to get your condition correctly diagnosed by a doctor and discuss an appropriate treatment plan, doctors are often not the best people to talk to. Not because they don't understand (they do) and not because they don't care (they do); but because doctors simply don't have the time, given the number of patients they have to see during surgery hours – whether on a private or public basis. I think the need to talk and be listened to, without fear of judgement, is vital to recovery and is certainly one of the reasons therapy is such an effective treatment for depression. *(You can read more about treatments and counselling in Chapter 2.)*

While researching this book, I came across a very good explanation about the importance of talking to someone. It centred round what is known as "circular logic" – a logic that often takes someone else to make you understand that how you are thinking is not logical. "*This*

*kind of logic is like having one shoe nailed to the floor and
running at top speed: the faster you go, the dizzier you get.
It never occurs to you to sit down, untie your shoes, step out
of them, and walk off barefoot in some new direction . . .
Sometimes it takes talking to someone besides yourself to
break out of circular logic, someone who is on the outside
looking in.*" (Dr Paul Quinnett, QPR Institute).

The trip proved to be a tonic in more ways than one
and I was grateful to my friend for booking it, even
though she knew there was a risk I would pull out at the
last minute. I felt myself relaxing for the first time in well
over a year. In fact, the first paragraphs of this book were
penned on the plane on the way home. True, all the
financial problems were still there and I would continue
to battle the ramifications, but I was alive and now I was
able to put things into perspective.

I first discussed writing a book about my illness with
my son. As he was the person who most bore witness to
the brunt of my depression and the final months, I wanted
to know what he thought. I knew that, at almost twenty-
one, he would be able to grasp the implications and his
views were important to me. He was candid in discussing
it with me and, since then, we have had many discussions
about depression, stigma and a host of other related
issues. He was happy for me to do it; but only on the
condition I would honestly portray the nightmare of my
illness, however uncomfortable it may be.

I gave him my word that I would write openly and
honestly, and I ran chapters and ideas by him and Gerry
constantly for their opinions. The rest of the family

unanimously supported my idea and shared the belief that, until somebody stood up and admitted to being depressed, the stigma which surrounds the illness will never be eradicated and people will never have a real insight into how debilitating depression can be, not only for the sufferer, but also for those who care about them. As you will read elsewhere in this book, I hold strong views about stigma. I believe it is perpetuated through misconception and borne by a lack of education. Stigma is the fault of the ignorant – not of the sufferer, who is deeply affected by it.

Very early on I made an altruistic decision in relation to this book. As I was the person who elected to go public in the hope of highlighting awareness of the hell that is depression, I was going to shield my family from it as much as possible. Yes, by virtue of association, they would be intrinsically linked with the book, but I felt that there was no need for them to be put under what would inevitably be an uncomfortable spotlight. They have been through enough; they lived through events in this book with me, and also the many events that are not in this book, and I feel they have a right to some privacy.

My family were delighted that I was writing again, though they never doubted my ability like I did. They could see past the illness, when I was blinded by it. They knew the person who had been enveloped by depression, and they, and Gerry in particular, fought hard to get me back. I have finally returned from the dark place I was in; a place I will never again return to. I've looked at life from both sides now and I am very glad I have.

EPILOGUE

**"Our greatest glory is not in never falling,
but in rising every time we fall."**

CONFUCIUS

These days, I am secure in the knowledge that I will never again suffer in the way I did, for those life circumstances could never replicate themselves. I now know that the unmanageable mess that depression usually creates doesn't become manageable; it just becomes more unmanageable. Some people have asked if I have found writing this book therapeutic, or if I have written it as a way of exorcising the ghosts of my illness. The answer is, no. It is my way – without being evangelical or hypocritical – of being vocal about something not usually spoken about; my way of being able to say to the hundreds of thousands of people who felt and continue to feel as I did, that, "You know what? It's okay to feel like this. It doesn't make you mad and it doesn't make you any less of a person." Depression is not a fault or a failure; it is an illness, which can strike any person at any time, irrespective of social or economic status.

Who knows what forces combine to make us the people we are? Some say genetics, some say environment – the "Nature versus Nurture" debate will always be argued. Personally, I believe that we inherit certain traits through genetics, while the skills to cope with life and its trials and tribulations are learned skills that we acquire through experience. Equally, I believe that depression occurs more as a result of a life-event or environment, than it does through genetics. I can find research that supports my view, and I can find research that disagrees with it, but then depression is often subjective.

Hearing my family's experience of my illness and, in particular, my children's experiences, was very painful to listen to. There were very many times I did not recognise myself as the person they were speaking about. I was so very thankful that their love for me is, as mine is for them, utterly unconditional. It was with a wry smile that I wrote the statistic, "For every one case of depression, an average of five people will be directly affected." There are five people in my immediate family (including my mother and sister).

I thought long and hard before writing this book, and indeed many times while actually writing it. As an extremely private person, I asked myself time and time again, if I really wanted to expose myself in such a radical way. To be honest, I didn't really. I didn't relish being put under scrutiny, of making my very private world so very public. I knew there were going to be some people who would think I was mad writing a book like this.

However, the reasons I would choose not to write it are the very reasons depression is the epidemic and silent illness it is today. I was in a position, through my ability to write, to be able to put a "face" to depression, so to speak. To stand up, with my head held high, and say,

"Yes, I was depressed, and it is nothing to be ashamed of or embarrassed by." Looking at my photo, I wondered if people could tell by looking at me that I was depressed. Although I thought it highly unlikely, I didn't know. In fact, I still don't know. Do you? What does a depressed person "*look*" like?

Yes, it would be uncomfortable going under the spotlight, but the alternative was – as so many people are forced to, through shame, embarrassment, denial and fear – simply to remain silent and not talk about it. To have to deny you are ill and unable to cope is difficult. To be made – through the ignorance of stigma – to feel like a twenty-first-century pariah and social outcast is even more difficult and one of the reasons this illness is so under-reported. Those who stigmatise depression are no doubt unaware of the fact that one in four of them will also battle with this illness. With any other illness, you wouldn't think twice about going to your GP to get something to make you well again. Depression should be no different; but it is.

I recently read an account of depression in which the author says that to stigmatise an illness is odious. Like me, she wished that she hadn't spent so long trying to manage because of shame, which retrospectively became ignorance. This is probably the single biggest reason why so many people who are depressed struggle on without asking for help, myself included.

In many ways I am a very different person to the person I was before my illness, but in other ways I haven't changed an iota. Mostly, I look back at the past few years with sadness, rather than bitterness. Many of the lessons

I learned came at too great a price, but all contributed to make me the person I am today.

Depression is an illness from which we learn and we grow. It is not a life sentence, nor is it incurable. It is one of the most common emotional problems and it is a "sometime" thing that will run its course and from which you will recover. Being depressed doesn't make you mad, it makes you sick; and whatever you may think at the time, you are not alone. Over four hundred thousand people are going through the very same thing on any given day in this country and many, many millions more around the world.

I have also been asked, if I could, would I turn back the clock and not have had depression? This is a little more difficult to answer because I am conscious of the hurt, the pain, and the confusion my illness – and my actions during it – caused to my family. However, even taking this into account, my answer is, no; I wouldn't change it. I have learned invaluable lessons from depression that I would not otherwise have learned. I have a far greater understanding of the complexities of depression and far more respect now for those who battle it day in, day out, in an effort to beat it. I've always had an interest in the workings of the brain and depression has taught me that sometimes we may think we know about something from theory when, in truth, we know nothing at all.

I am now in the throes of writing my next book about the organ retention scandal in Ireland, which will be published by Poolbeg Press in February 2009. It is another issue that will invoke much emotion and public debate, but it is also an issue that has largely been brushed under the carpet. Are people ready to hear about the organs of deceased children being left to rot in buckets? Of sand being put into the bodies of children to make up the weight of missing organs? Of organs being incinerated like clinical waste without the knowledge of parents? I highly doubt it, because it is something that is not only shocking, but also unpleasant and uncomfortable to have to deal with. However, I, and the many thousands of people in Ireland who have been affected by organ retention, continue to suffer the horrific consequences and aftermath of it to this day, coupled with a government that not only has done little to help, but also has withdrawn what little funding had been made available.

I am hesitant to say I am "cured" of depression because it lends itself to connotations that are often subjective and, more importantly, downright incorrect. I got sick and I got better; just as if I had had a broken limb that took time to heal, or a pain I had to take pain relief for. What I can say is the road to recovery is a long one upon which I am still travelling but I am no longer drowning in an emotional whirlpool, nor am I battling apathy. Depression may be a state of mind that very often incapacitates a person, but when you come out the other side of it you realise you are capable of anything and are a far stronger and more empathetic person because of it.

Although I will never joke about what I have gone through – actually, this is not quite true and I have purposely left this line in rather than edit it out. When reading the proofs, my sister (who is a healthcare professional) reminded me about the times we joked about my illness, simply as an escape; a brief moment of light relief. Indeed, a Dutch friend of mine, Michel, who also shares my dark sense of humour, would often text me things that, to most people, would seem entirely inappropriate and offensive to my illness. As I recovered, some of the emails that passed between us would certainly have caused people to question my "friends" and my professional credibility! We have always been like this during times of crises. However, on a more serious note, we have had many serious discussions over the years and I knew that, if I needed him, I had only to pick up the phone and he would be on the first flight over.

These days I write in solitude in my comfortable office, usually with our dog, Sam, lying faithfully at my feet. By the time this book launches, my next book will be finished and I have drafted a tentative outline for the one I plan to write after that. I also want to get back to writing a newspaper column. I may be alone, but I am no longer lonely.

I take pleasure now from simple things in life, which are things we often miss with life's frantic pace. I'm far more laid back and philosophical . . . most of the time anyway! Much of what I previously considered to be important actually matters little in the grand scheme of things. What's important is your family, your health and your friends; things we often take for granted and never truly appreciate until we don't have them.

I have learned to accept my illness for what it was. It is not something I dwell on, for it taught me what I needed to know, yet I never want to forget it, or become desensitised about it. I believe that part of any healing process is to look forward, not back. We cannot change the past, but we can shape the future. Recently I saw a plaque in a shop that appealed to my dry sense of humour. I couldn't resist buying it and it now hangs in my office. It reads: "Welcome to the Funny Farm". Normal? What's normal?!

2

Understanding Depression

**"He who does not understand your silence will
probably not understand your words."**

ELBERT HUBBARD

Depression is an illness that affects over 400,000 people
in Ireland every year. It will affect one in three of us at
some time in our lives, either directly or indirectly through a
family member or friend. It remains an unreported illness,
primarily due to fear of being labelled or stigmatised. A
sufferer will commonly experience feelings of shame,
embarrassment and isolation, largely as a result of the
way depression is wrongly perceived by society through a
lack of education and understanding. In order to address
this problem, it must first be understood.

What is Depression?

Depression means different things to different people. Its
causes and symptoms vary enormously and it affects
people in many different ways. For example, depression
may be expressed in different ways according to age, sex

and culture. However, and it is important to note, depression pervades all ages, cultures and socio-economic backgrounds.

A woman who is depressed will most likely display different symptoms to a teenager or elderly man. Equally, the latter will exhibit different symptoms to those that may affect a woman. If depression is to be understood and more recognisable, then it is important to be aware of all the different types and symptoms.

Statistics show that women are three times more likely to suffer from depression than men. However, it must be taken into account that many things are included in the figure for women. Hormonal factors play a huge part and some women suffer from physiology-based types of depression that men cannot suffer from. These include premenstrual syndrome, postpartum depression and peri-menopausal depression. Women are also more likely to suffer from Seasonal Affective Disorder (SAD).

Depression is universal; by typing the word into search engine Google, you will be given the option of 72,100,000 results, compared with 24,000,000 for heart disease in the same search engine. That's how common depression is, but it also is an indication of just how much information there is on the illness. True, you will have to sift through thousands of specialist websites, but many are user-friendly and explain the condition in easily understood terms. However, it should be noted that the internet is no substitute for professional medical advice and diagnosis.

We all go through highs and lows in our moods and it is quite normal to feel unhappy or low from time to time. There are few people who have never suffered from a dose of "the blues" or feeling down in the dumps, particularly after receiving bad news or when things are just not going well. However, this mood usually passes in a few days. Suffering from "the blues" is not the same as experiencing depression, or "clinical depression" as it is sometimes called.

The symptoms of depression include a sense of hopelessness, worthlessness, tiredness, disinterest in everyday things and despair. Generally, people suffering from depression find it difficult to cope with life. The feeling of gloom persists and interferes with the ability to work, study, eat, sleep and enjoy life in general. Although depression can occur at any age, it is most prevalent in people aged twenty-two to forty-four and should always be taken seriously. It is estimated that around 15 per cent of people who are severely depressed will take their own lives by committing suicide.

Depression in older people is common, but it is often missed because of the misconception that it is normal for older people to feel down. Although old people usually experience more bereavement, physical illness and social isolation than young people, depression is *not* part of the ageing process. Like anyone else who is depressed, it is important that an older person seeks help from their doctor *(see Chapter 6)*.

Depression is very treatable and statistics show that the vast majority of people who suffer with depression can be successfully treated with the right support. It usually lasts from weeks to several months, but the common thread for all is that recovery from an illness takes time and the return to "normal life" brings its own set of challenges.

The key to recovery from depression is first to accept the problem and then seek the appropriate treatment and help. As depression has varied signs and symptoms, which range from mild to moderate, it is important to know what to look for. Knowing what to spot is very often the first step in understanding and overcoming the illness.

Signs and Symptoms

Feeling depressed and actually suffering from depression are two entirely different things. It's easy to "feel" depressed after a bad day or after a disappointment, but this passes in a few days and you pick yourself up, learn from the experience and move on. However, the utter desolation, despondency and isolation of clinical depression are relentless and uncompromising. It is often likened to living in a "black hole" or under a "dark cloud of gloom". In my story, I describe my experience of depression as freefalling into an abyss so deep it threatened to quickly swallow me. There was no escaping my feeling of despair.

However, it should be noted that, in some cases, people with depression feel very little. They don't feel particularly sad; they don't feel particularly despairing. In fact, they often feel nothing. For them, life is empty. They lose the ability to feel, to experience happiness or pleasure. They become apathetic and go through the motions without feeling anything.

"I remember feeling nothing, and that's what surprised me most. I just went through the motions day in, day out. I'd go out with friends and not be able to enjoy myself. I lost interest in all the things I used to enjoy, but still did them anyway, hoping I would start to feel something again. I couldn't see a future for myself and just concentrated on getting through one day at a time. This continued for weeks. I thought that to be depressed you had to feel depressed, which is what confused me. It was only after speaking to my GP that I realised that the symptoms I had were those of depression."

PAULA, 31

Signs and symptoms vary from person to person. However, there are quite a number that are recognised as being signs of depression. The World Health Organisation defines clinical depression as:

- Two weeks of an abnormal depressed mood
- Loss of interest or pleasure in activities that used to be enjoyable
- Reduced energy or feeling tired

87

- Loss of confidence and self-esteem
- Feeling guilty and unworthy
- Recurrent thoughts of death or suicide, or any suicidal/self-harming behaviour
- Reduced ability to think or concentrate
- Agitated or slow movements
- Disturbed sleep (not enough/too much/poor quality)
- Change in appetite (increase or decrease) with weight change
- Decreased libido
- Unexplained physical symptoms.

Minor depression includes two of the first three symptoms and at least two others.

Moderate depression includes two of the first three symptoms and at least four others.

Severe depression includes all three of the first three symptoms and at least five others.

Aware, the Irish organisation that supports those suffering from and affected by depression, has developed an acronym, "FESTIVAL", for symptoms and it features in much of their literature. It is an easy way both to learn and to remember some of the most common signs and symptoms of depression. Aware draws attention to the fact that sometimes you don't have to *feel* depressed to *be* depressed. They advise that if five or more of the FESTIVAL symptoms are present for two weeks or more, to see your GP.

- **F**eeling — depressed, sad, anxious or bored
- **E**nergy — tired, fatigued, everything an effort, slowed movements
- **S**leep — waking during the night or too early in the morning, oversleeping, or trouble going to sleep
- **T**hinking — slow thinking, poor concentration, forgetful or indecisive
- **I**nterest — loss of interest in food, work, sex, and life seems dull
- **V**alue — reduced sense of self-worth, low self-esteem, or guilt
- **A**ches — headaches, chest, or other pains without a physical basis
- **L**ive — not wanting to live, suicidal thoughts or thinking of death

Types of Depression

There are several different types of depressive disorders, each with overlapping symptoms. However, each type has distinct signs and symptoms, which are unique to that particular depression.

Major Depression

This depression is characterised by persistent feelings of sadness and an inability to experience pleasure. These symptoms are constant and interfere with the ability to function productively and enjoy life. If major depression is left untreated, an episode generally lasts for about six months. Although some people may experience just a single episode of depression in their lifetime, it is more common for major depression to recur. Major depression is looked at further throughout this chapter.

Atypical Depression

This is a common subtype of major depression, which features distinct symptoms. A sufferer tends to react positively or negatively to external events by feeling either very depressed or quite hopeful, depending what the situation is. For example, temporary mood lifts are quite common particularly after doing something that is fun or when out with friends. However, this good feeling doesn't last long and once they are alone they quickly slip back into depression.

People with atypical depression tend to overeat and oversleep as well as exhibit signs of hypersensitivity, making them extremely sensitive to rejection by someone who is close to them. A frequent complaint is that of a very heavy feeling in the limbs and an increased desire for comfort food such as chocolate. In addition to having typical symptoms of depression, a person should have two of the following four symptoms for a diagnosis of atypical depression to be considered:

- Leaden feeling in the arms and legs
- Needing excessive amounts of sleep (hypersomnia)
- History of interpersonal rejection sensitivity
- Increased appetite and weight gain

Research shows that atypical depression is effectively treated with anti-depressants, such as selective serotonin re-uptake inhibitors, which are commonly referred to as SSRIs (see anti-depressant medications in the section dealing with treatments for depression). As with other depressions, a person may also respond well to therapy.

Reactive Depression

As its name suggests, this type of depression is usually a temporary depression that occurs as an emotional response to a stressful life event or loss. It is the most frequently experienced mood change. As individuals we react differently to situations, so this type of depression can be in response to a great number of things. Contrary to what some people may think, reactive depression is perfectly normal and only becomes abnormal when the reaction becomes disproportionate to the event, or when it takes longer than it should to go away.

In practically all cases, the contributory cause is easily identifiable. It is for this reason that with this type of depression much emphasis is placed on resolving the cause as opposed to the symptom (depression). For example, your job may be the cause of reactive depression. You may be getting bullied, harassed or even passed over for promotion, causing feelings of sadness and resentment. The solution to the depression, in this instance, may be seriously to consider changing job and thus removing yourself from the situation that is causing the depression.

Unlike more severe forms of depression, although sufferers will often feel low, angry or anxious and may have trouble sleeping, they often get relief from their symptoms by engaging in social or activity interests and, more often than not, see work as a welcome distraction. Essentially, this type of depression, as a rule, doesn't interfere to any great extent with a person's ability to live life relatively normally.

As the causes are largely dependant on an individual's perception of and reaction to a given situation, they are impossible to list. Suffice to say they range from something going wrong in work or not making the grade in something, through to separation, divorce and bereavement. The length of an episode of reactive depression depends on the severity of the perceived loss and can last from a few days to several months. However, in certain cases, such as death of a loved one, it can last up to years. However, a person will not be depressed all this time and will have increasing periods without depression as the sense of grief lessens. Although there will sometimes be raw emotions to deal with and adjustments that may need to be made, generally the person is not affected for very long and the symptoms tend to disappear mostly of their own accord as the person learns to deal with whatever caused the depression.

Dysthymia

This is also referred to as "Dysthymic Disorder" and is a type of low-grade depression that lasts for sustained periods of at least two years. Although it is less severe than major depression, its symptoms prevent people from enjoying life to the fullest. Lethargy, sleep disturbance and loss of appetite are often experienced. One of the most common telltale signs of dysthymia is that you will be mildly to moderately depressed on more days than you are not. It is also common to have normal moods for brief periods. Often sufferers will remark that they cannot recall a time when they did not feel depressed. Quite a lot of people with dysthymia also experience major depressive episodes – a condition termed "double depression".

Dysthymia affects two to three women for every man and is thought to begin in childhood and adolescence. Treatments vary but commonly include a combination of anti-depressants and counselling/psychotherapy. Dysthymia shares many of the common symptoms associated with other types of depression. It causes changes in behaviour, feelings, thinking and also physical changes. Symptoms may last for months and not all need to be present to be suffering from this type of depression. A good indicator is if some of the symptoms have persisted for most of the time for up to two years. These include:

- Difficulty concentrating and making decisions
- Negative thinking
- Poor self-esteem/self-criticism

- Pervading feeling of sadness for no apparent reason

- Lack of motivation

- Irritability

- Feelings of despair and hopelessness

- Social withdrawal

- Changes in weight

- Disturbed sleep

- Physical symptoms such as aches and pains

Treatment

As with other types of depression, treatment for dysthymia usually comprises anti-depressants and/or therapy and again, SSRIs are the most commonly prescribed medication. Therapy is often very effective and is used to treat this condition in several ways. One-to-one supportive counselling addresses the feelings of despair and hopelessness and supports the person. Highly-popular cognitive therapy helps a person to differentiate between problems that are critical and those that are minor. It helps to change the depressed person's opinion by tackling feelings of self-doubt, and also deals with possibly unrealistic expectations. A third facet of counselling is problem-solving, whereby the concentration is on changing things in a person's life that are stressful. Left untreated, dysthymia normally continues with a person through life.

Tips for dealing with Dysthymia

- If you think you may be suffering from this, talk to your doctor, who will be able to start you on a course of treatment – there is no need to suffer in silence.

- Learn how to recognise the symptoms.

- Take plenty of regular exercise.

- Make an effort to do things you enjoy.

- Eat a well-balanced diet.

- Avoid drugs and alcohol as these make depression worse.

Seasonal Affective Disorder (SAD)

Ireland ranks highly when it comes to countries with large numbers of people affected by SAD. Studies rank Ireland near the top, with one in five of our population affected by SAD. In the UK, one in fifty people suffer from it. Research shows that SAD becomes more common the further you are away from the equator. This indicates that it is linked to the change in the number of daylight hours through the year and explains why it is more common in northern climates.

Although many people have heard of SAD, it is not always thought of as a major depression. It is not uncommon for people who suffer from recurring bouts of depression to show a seasonal disorder. SAD is a major depression that has a seasonal pattern and most commonly occurs in the autumn or winter when the amount of sunlight is limited.

You can develop SAD at any age, but the condition is most prevalent in people aged eighteen to thirty, with twice as many women as men affected. The risk of getting SAD for the first time goes down as you age.

Symptoms tend to start with the onset of autumn, are at their worst during the shortest daylight months and then improve and disappear when spring arrives. It can be a difficult type of depression to diagnose because it shares symptoms that are common with other types of depression. However, there are things that suggest you may be suffering from SAD, such as suffering from the same symptoms for two or more consecutive years, or only feeling low primarily during winter months.

Symptoms

SAD has some unique symptoms, which include:

- Extreme fatigue: often feeling very drowsy during the day.

- Sleeping excessively: waking up feeling tired and wanting to go to bed early.

- Lethargy: often losing interest in usual hobbies and activities.

- Overeating: particularly craving high carbohydrate foods such as bread and pasta.

- Weight gain: due mainly to carbohydrate cravings.

- Mood: feelings of anxiety, irritability and disinterest are common.

Diagnosis

Although SAD can sometimes be difficult to diagnose, in addition to looking at lifestyle, eating and sleeping patterns, and behaviour, there are certain things that can speed diagnosis. Although your GP will carry out a physical and psychological examination, knowing what unique things to look for often helps to distinguish SAD from other types of depression. These may include:

- Experiencing the same symptoms at the same time of year for more than two consecutive years.

- If you only get depressed during these times and not during other months of the year.

- There are no obvious psychological or environmental causes for your depression.

- A close relative – a parent, brother or sister – has had SAD.

Treatment

As with all types of depression, there are a numbers of treatments for SAD and it is not uncommon to have to use a combination of treatments to get the best results. Again, your GP will discuss all the options and advise what is best for you. The most common treatments for SAD are:

Light Therapy

This kind of therapy is a very popular and effective way of treating SAD. Light therapy is easy to use, is effective for two out of three people and has few side effects. An improvement is usually apparent after about a week, though it may take longer for some people. A rule of thumb is that, if after six weeks you notice no difference, then light therapy is probably not a suitable treatment. There are essentially two types of light therapy: Bright light treatment, which involves sitting in front of a "light box" that mimics outdoor light for a given period every day; and dawn stimulation, which is a dim light that comes on near where you sleep and gets brighter over time. It mimics a sunrise and most often comes in the form of an alarm clock. Both of these things are readily available to purchase.

It is, however, very important not to try to make homemade or improvised versions of these – for example, shining a bright light in your eyes or using a tanning bed is not recommended because, quite apart from not working or being effective in treating the condition, you run a high risk of damaging your eyes or your skin. Light therapy equipment is clinically and medically designed and is specialist equipment designed to treat SAD. You need to use the light therapy every day during the months you normally get depressed or you run the risk of it not working and depression recurring.

Anti-depressants

With more severe symptoms it is also normal for your doctor to prescribe anti-depressants, which is likely to be a selective serotonin re-uptake inhibitor (SSRI). These work by increasing the level of serotonin in the brain, which is the chemical that affects mood. They are slow release, so it may take between two to four weeks to start feeling their effects. They are not addictive and are generally only taken during the months of depression. It is important not to stop taking these suddenly without consulting your doctor, because of the risk of side effects. When it is time to stop, your doctor will gradually lessen the dose to reduce the risk of problems.

Counselling

Some people find it helpful to talk about their condition or enlist assistance in helping them to cope with its symptoms. Counselling also helps to educate you about the symptoms and the most effective way of managing them. A counsellor will also draw up a self-help plan, designed to help you deal with stress and anxiety in a positive way. Again, your GP will be able to advise on what's available.

Things you can do to reduce the symptoms of SAD

- Be open with people about your condition – it is better that family and friends understand what is wrong with you and lend their support

- Eat a balanced diet – you will have an increased desire for carbohydrates

- Learn about relaxation techniques and breathing exercises

- Get as much natural sunlight as possible – preferably by going outside

- Look at ways of maximising natural light in your home

- Exercise and keep active

- Avoid stress where possible

- Read up and inform yourself about your condition

Postnatal Depression

Postnatal depression (PND) affects about one in ten new mothers in Ireland, a figure that, according to Madge Fogarty, chairwoman of Post Natal Depression Ireland, is rising, without enough provision being made to support and educate women. Ms Fogarty maintains that there continues to be a makeshift approach when it comes to treating PND, citing over-stretched health nurses who are under-educated about PND and also an over-dependence on medication to treat the problem. "People need to realise that there is help out there if they need it."

Having a baby is a huge life-event. Pregnancy and the year following birth can be stressful times for both parents. The symptoms of postnatal depression (PND) vary and often a woman will be unaware she is actually suffering from depression and instead attribute how she is feeling to being part and parcel of having a new baby. Some of the most common things women complain of include feelings of tiredness, irritability, sleeplessness, loss of appetite and anxiety. PND usually develops soon after childbirth, but can also take months to develop. It usually lasts about three months and nearly always disappears by the time the baby is a year old.

Although it is generally accepted that there are two forms of PND, I think there are actually three: baby blues, postnatal depression and puerperal psychosis, which are all different. As symptoms of PND are not always obvious to a new mother, it is important that partners and families know what to look for, so they can assist the mother in getting help sooner rather than later.

Baby Blues

Getting the "baby blues" is very common after childbirth. It is often the cause of feeling low and it is the least severe type of PND. According to Postnatal Depression Ireland, it is a very temporary condition usually lasting around forty-eight hours and generally disappears of its own accord without needing treatment.

Postnatal Depression

PND usually develops in the weeks immediately following childbirth, though it can also take months to develop. Common symptoms include:

- Feeling low: feeling miserable and getting little pleasure from anything.

- Feeling irritable: snapping at people, most often your partner and family.

- Feeling unable to cope: everything is overwhelming, a feeling you can do nothing right often accompanied by a feeling of inadequacy.

- Feeling clingy: needing constant reassurance from people.

- Feeling anxious: worried about your own health, worrying excessively that something is going to happen your baby. According to Post Natal Depression Ireland, anxiety can be acute and often takes the form of being afraid to be alone with the baby, who you fear might scream the place down or not feed or choke or be dropped or harmed in some other way. Some depressed mothers perceive the baby as "it"; instead of feeling that they have given birth to the loveliest, most adorable creature in the world, they feel detached from the infant. They can't see that their baby is all that beautiful – indeed, they may find their baby a rather strange, mysterious little being, whose thoughts (if any) can't be fathomed and whose unpredictable needs and emotions have somehow to be satisfied. The task of a new mother who hasn't yet "fallen in love" with her baby is extremely difficult. The love comes in the end, but usually when the baby is older and more interesting.

However, Post Natal Depression Ireland points out that "PND may develop even when a mother's love is strong. The mother then worries desperately in case she should lose her precious baby through infection, mishandling, faulty development or a 'cot death'. Snuffles cause her terrible worry, she frets over how much weight has been (or not been) gained, she is alarmed if the baby is crying or if it is too silent – has its breathing stopped? She wants constant reassurance from her partner, the Health Visitor, the doctor, her family, the woman next door – anyone really."

Your GP or health visitor will be able to determine whether you are suffering from PND and will be able to suggest treatments.

Postnatal psychosis

Postnatal psychosis – also known as puerperal psychosis (puerperal refers to the six-week period immediately following childbirth) – is a rare but severe form of depression affecting about one in 500 women. It is biological in nature and, like any psychosis, is a severe mental illness, which affects a person's ability to relate to reality. Symptoms can include irrational behaviour, confusion and suicidal thoughts. Women with postnatal psychosis often need specialist psychiatric treatment and hospitalisation because, in addition to possible thoughts of suicide, she will most likely suffer from bouts of extreme depression and extreme elation, during which time it is not possible to look after her baby. However, due to medical advances, the average duration of this illness is a few weeks with a complete recovery.

Common causes of PND

As with any type of depression, there is no single cause responsible and it can happen to anyone. There are, however, certain things known to be contributory factors. These include:

Social circumstances: Lack of a supportive and caring partner has been cited as one of the most likely causes of PND. Additionally, isolation from close family and recent traumatic events also fall into this category.

Previous depression: Women who have had previous psychological problems may have difficulty adjusting to the constant demands and responsibilities of a new baby.

Birth experience: according to PND Ireland, some women may feel that their birth experience failed to match up to their expectations. The feeling of being "let down" can cause depression.

Finances: according to Aware, some studies suggest socio-economic difficulties are also a risk factor.

Changes in Lifestyle: The birth of a baby brings irrevocable changes to a new mother's life. New babies are hard work, with the constant demands of crying, feeding, bathing and putting to sleep. This usually means a significant loss of uninterrupted sleep. The new mother is suddenly responsible twenty-four hours a day. The birth of the baby can have a profound impact on relationships, which can be put under enormous strain. A new mother loses the freedom she enjoyed before the baby arrived. This sense of loss can cause depression unless the mother can find ways of adjusting to her profound changes in lifestyle. PND Ireland also cites illness before the birth and working right up until the birth as other common causes.

Treatment of Postnatal Depression

It appears that counselling and, in particular, Cognitive Behavioural Therapy, is effective in treating this type of depression.

As with other types of depression, it may (though by no means always) be treated with medication such as SSRIs.

Support groups such as PND Ireland and the many others that are on the web can be a great way of interacting with other people who are in the same situation, as well as giving very practical advice and tips on how best to deal with your situation.

Coping with Postnatal Depression

The demands of a new baby are constant and the impact on a new mother and indeed a couple can be huge. There is only so much preparation that can be done to get ready for a new baby and for the changes that will ensue. However, as is often the case, the reality can often be different to the textbooks. There are a number of "dos and don'ts" when it comes to coping with a new baby, which can help enormously.

Dos and Don'ts

- **Do** sleep when your baby sleeps, or, if this is not possible because of other children, aim to rest.

- **Don't** be afraid to ask for and to accept help.

- **Do** enlist the help of your partner to alternate night feeds immediately if you are bottle-feeding, and, if you are breast-feeding, after the first few weeks (to avoid nipple confusion for the baby). Breast milk can be successfully expressed for this purpose.

- **Don't** fret over trivial things that may not get done in the early weeks as you adapt.

- **Do** attend your post-natal visit, even if you don't think you need to.

- **Don't** worry about previous routines; you'll soon establish new ones.

- **Do** try to make "me" time by enlisting the help of friends and family to baby-sit.

- **Don't** let your diet suffer; a balanced diet is important at this time.

- **Do** talk to someone about any worries or concerns you may have.

- **Don't** add stress to the equation by trying to do everything and failing.

- **Do** try to make time as a couple, get out for dinner or go to the cinema.

Bipolar Disorder (Manic Depression)

The main characteristic of this type of depression is that the symptoms of major depression are alternated with episodes of mania. Typically, the switch from one dramatic mood extreme to the other is gradual, with each manic or depressive episode lasting for days, weeks or months. Although the term "elation" would suggest it is an experience based largely on pleasure, quite the opposite is true.

Episodes of mania and depression typically recur throughout a person's life, with symptom-free periods between episodes. Approximately one-third of sufferers will have some residual symptoms. Bipolar disorder is highly disruptive to everyday functioning and negatively affects energy, activity levels, judgement and behaviour.

Common symptoms of a manic episode

- Feelings of heightened energy, creativity and euphoria
- Rapid speech to the extent that others cannot keep up or understand what the person is saying
- Erratic behaviour, e.g. gambling savings, promiscuity, getting into debt
- Impulsive/irrational decisions, e.g. quitting a job
- Acting recklessly without consideration of consequences
- Racing thoughts; flitting from one idea to another in rapid succession
- Reduced need for sleep e.g. sleeping very little, but feeling very energetic
- Hyperactivity
- Unrealistic beliefs about one's abilities
- Impaired judgement
- Feelings of being powerful, invincible, etc
- Feeling extremely high or extremely irritable

- Aggressiveness
- Anger at those who may comment on their behaviour
- Denial that anything is wrong

Aware has also developed a FESTIVAL acronym for the symptoms of mania:

Feeling   elated, enthusiastic, excited, angry, irritable or depressed

Energy   great energy "never felt as well", over-talkative or over-active

Sleep   reduced need for sleep and marked difficulty in getting off to sleep

Thinking   racing thoughts, "pressure in the head", indecisive, jumping from one topic to another, poor concentration

Interest   increased interest in pleasurable activities, new adventures, sex, alcohol, street drugs, religion, music or art

Value   excessive and unrealistic belief in one's ability or having grandiose plans

Aches   never tiring, being unaware of the physical symptoms of illness such as asthma, having muscle tension at the back of the head or around the shoulders

Live   thinking that one can live forever, taking reckless physical risks or, if angry or distressed, feeling suicidal

If five or more of the above symptoms are present for more than two weeks, it may be a manic episode.

Although the depressive phase of bipolar disorder is very similar to major depression, there are some obvious differences. Bipolar depression is more likely to include symptoms of low energy, where the person tends to move and speak slowly and sleep a lot. Additionally, they are also more prone to having a "psychotic depression" in which they lose contact with reality.

Common symptoms of a depressive episode

- Often won't get out of bed
- Feelings of sadness, emptiness, shame, guilt and self-loathing
- Disinterest in things
- Thoughts of death or suicide
- Fatigue
- No energy
- Physical and mental sluggishness
- Appetite or weight changes
- Sleep disruption
- Concentration problems

Causes
Most scientists agree that there is no single cause for bipolar disorder. As bipolar disorder tends to run in families, some people are genetically predisposed to it. However, not

everyone with this inherited risk develops the illness. This would suggest that external factors also play a role in the development of bipolar disorder. Some of the most common triggers of bipolar disorder include those listed below. However, it is important to note that episodes of mania or depression can occur without any obvious triggers.

Common triggers for bipolar disorder

- Emotional trauma
- Stress
- Major life events (good and bad)
- Substance abuse – hard drugs such as cocaine, ecstasy and amphetamines can trigger mania, while alcohol and tranquilisers can trigger a depressive episode
- Sleep deprivation
- Seasonal changes – research shows that episodes of mania are more common during the summer, while depressive episodes are more common during autumn, winter and spring
- Sudden change – such as moving house or starting a new job

Treatments

As with most types of depression, people with bipolar disorder can lead productive lives with the right treatment – including those who are severely affected. As bipolar disorder is a recurrent illness, long-term treatment is almost always used, mostly as a preventive measure. Additionally, a treatment plan that combines medication and psychosocial treatment is generally employed to manage the illness on a long-term basis. Without treatment, unlike other depressions, bipolar disorder tends to worsen over time with symptoms becoming more severe, more frequent and more manic/depressive with time.

A psychiatrist (who is also qualified to prescribe medication) generally decides on a treatment plan for a patient with bipolar disorder. One of the most common ways of treating and controlling this disorder is with medications known as "mood stabilisers". Mostly, this treatment continues for extended periods (years). During episodes of mania or depression other medications may be added, for a shorter time, to treat these episodes. As with all medications, possible side effects and contra-indications should be thoroughly discussed with your doctor before commencing them.

Common Causes and Risk Factors for Depresson

There is no single cause of depression. Research shows that early life experience, genetic predisposition, lifestyle factors and certain personality traits all play a part in causing depression. It is sometimes preceded by a setback in life. However, something that causes depression in one person may have no effect on another.

There are a number of risk factors, which are known to contribute to the onset of depression. For example, people who are isolated and have few friends or family members to turn to in times of stress are more likely to develop depression. Additionally, statistics show that if you've been clinically depressed before, you're at a higher risk of becoming depressed again. Some of the most common risk factors include:

- Bereavement
- Financial worries
- Marital or relationship problems
- Alcohol or drug abuse
- Social isolation
- Stressful life experiences
- Early childhood trauma or abuse
- Unemployment or underemployment
- Health problems or chronic pain
- Family history of depression

Treatments for Depression

If you think you or someone you care about has depression, it is important to seek professional help sooner rather than later. Depression is a very under-reported illness, which is sad, because it is very treatable. People tend not to seek help for reasons such as embarrassment, shame and fear of being labelled. Instead they choose to struggle alone with no relief from all the symptoms associated with depression. In my case, I struggled on for the best part of a year with varying degrees of competency before g

Retrospectively, had I known then wha

would have gone to the doctor after a few

saved myself from a year of hell.

Another reason to see a doctor is because some ot

illnesses can sometimes look like depression, which makes
it important to get a complete evaluation. Visiting the
doctor is more often than not the first step on the road to
recovery. Most people who take this step find it an
enormous relief to share the burden of their illness with
someone, without fear of being judged or frowned upon.
A GP's surgery is one of the few places where stigma
about depression does not exist.

Although you may think you are the only person in the
world to feel as you do, chances are your GP has seen it
all and heard it all before. There will be very little you can
say about depression that will shock a doctor. Additionally,
given the fact that one in three people will be affected by
depression at some time in their lives, chances are your
doctor may have experienced depression on a personal
level, as well as on a professional level.

Doctors are familiar with recognising the symptoms of
depression and most GPs will have experience of treating
it in children, teenagers, men, women and elderly people.
By asking specific questions about your mood, appetite,
energy levels, libido and sleep patterns, your doctor will
quickly be able to assess the severity of your depression.

They are also likely to ask personal questions about
events and circumstances in your life that may help

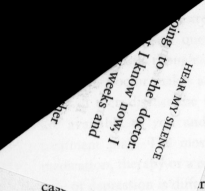

...ncing. Doctors are also ...about thoughts of self-...uicidal thoughts.

...nosis of depression, he or ...ous treatment options that ...tart you on a personalised ...common treatment involves ...ombination of the two. As each cas... ...rent, a treatment that works for one person ... ...tle benefit to another.

Therapy

It is becoming commonplace now for GPs to have in-house counsellors to help with depression and other emotional difficulties. It is usual for counsellors to have a background in mental heath nursing or a psychology-related field. Whether a counsellor attends at a doctor's practice or from a different place, a patient will see them on a regular basis, usually for a fixed number of sessions. Obviously, the number of sessions that may be needed are based on the needs of the patient and the type of treatment being offered by the counsellor.

Research suggests that use of medication and therapy together may be the most effective approach, particularly for more severe depressions. The reasoning is that while the medication provides relief from symptoms, therapy helps the person to learn about their illness and how best to manage it. There are many types of therapy used in the treatment of depression, with *cognitive behavioural therapy (CBT)* being the most popular. Other therapies include interpersonal therapy, behavioural therapy, psychodynamic therapy and family therapy. Group therapy is also quite common. However, a common link between all types of therapy is that the depressed person takes a proactive approach. The success of therapy depends on input from the person and it is not uncommon to be presented with exercises to do in between sessions. If the depression is so acute that it renders a person unable to interact, then therapy will not be of benefit until the individual starts to improve with medication.

Literally hundreds of studies have been conducted all over the world that support the effectiveness of CBT in the treatment of depression. American psychiatrist Aaron Beck is recognised as the father of CBT. In addition to writing many books and studies on this form of therapy, he also invented the widely used Beck Scales. Rather than dwell on the cause of the problem, CBT instead focuses on what the person can do immediately to help them to change how they are feeling.

CBT works on the premise that, for many people, depression is caused by faulty cognitions, e.g. an "all or nothing" mentality, misdirection of blame, etc. The person is then encouraged to start making notes of their thoughts throughout the day in an effort to understand how common and how often these thoughts occur every day. Discussion is then centred on these thoughts and also on the symptoms and behaviours of depression. The belief is that thoughts and behaviours are more likely to change emotions than dwelling on the past and what may or may not have caused the depression. This kind of therapy is relatively short term and usually lasts no longer than about twenty sessions, sometimes less. It works best for people who are quite distressed and upset by their depression and those who are willing to be open to new ways of thinking.

Interpersonal therapy, however, focuses on an individual's social relationships and ways of improving them. These skills will work on ways of improving the manner in which a person communicates and acts in various social and personal situations. Again, it is short term and is used on a one-to-one basis as well as within group therapy.

Family and couple therapy is usually suggested when a person's depression is so severe that it negatively impacts the dynamics and/or health of a close relationship(s).

Anti-depressant medications

Depression is commonly treated with anti-depressants. These have come a long way in the past couple of decades and there is now good evidence that these are not only effective, but also non-addictive. Although there is a wide range of these medications, depression is most often treated with *selective serotonin re-uptake inhibitors* (SSRIs).

These work by raising the levels of the natural chemical serotonin in the brain, which in turn tends to lift the mood. Although SSRIs work within a week of first taking them, it can take between four and six weeks to start feeling the full effects of them and seeing an improvement. You should continue taking them for at least six weeks before making a decision to stop taking them. You should always consult with your GP before ceasing.

Most people have only minor side effects, if any, after starting medication. These may include: diarrhoea, feeling sick, vomiting and headaches. Some people may develop a feeling of restlessness or mild anxiety. Minor side effects usually disappear in about a week. Your doctor will inform you fully of the potential side effects of any medication they intend prescribing for you, and if they don't, ask them about them.

SSRIs are not thought to be addictive. However, some people may have temporary withdrawal symptoms such as stomach upset or flu-like illness when treatment is first stopped. Your doctor will gradually reduce the dose as your treatment comes to an end to minimise or eliminate any side effects. SSRIs are usually taken for up to six months after you feel better and back to yourself. The reason for this is to prevent a recurrence.

Exercise

Exercise has been shown to be an effective way of treating depression and is a natural way to boost serotonin levels in the body. Although exercise may not be possible at the beginning, due to the symptoms of depression, it can be very beneficial once a person starts to feel a little better. I know that exercising was the last thing on my mind in the early days; I couldn't muster the strength to get out of bed, never mind get dressed and go out walking. However, as the depression started to lift, I started to go out for walks and felt better afterwards. There is a great sense of achievement after walking and it helps to blow away the cobwebs. Other things such as yoga, massage or relaxation techniques also help to lessen anxiety and are good stress-busters.

Complementary therapies

Complementary medicines and treatments may help in mild to moderate depression, but you must talk to your doctor about any treatments or supplements you intend to try. Herbal supplements may cause negative interactions with prescription medications or reduce their efficacy. As a rule, complementary medicines should not be substituted for traditional medical care and to rely solely on these to treat depression may not be effective enough.

Common symptoms of mild to moderate depression include: fatigue, headache, backache or unexplained aches and pains. Alternative therapies work on the principle of mind-body techniques, which are thought to strengthen the communication between your mind and your body. The most common techniques used to treat stress, anxiety and depression symptoms include:

- Acupuncture
- Relaxing and breathing exercises
- Yoga
- Meditation
- Tai chi
- Massage therapy

Susan's Story

Susan is twenty-nine years of age, single and went through a bout of depression, which lasted nine months, following a relationship break-up.

I had been going out with my boyfriend for two years, and living with him for one, when he came home from work one day and announced that he didn't love me anymore. He said it was nothing I had done and that he had just fallen out of love. I was knocked for six. There was no warning and it happened so suddenly that I didn't know how to react at first. I couldn't believe it. We were in love, or at least I thought we were. We had even discussed getting married and having children at some point in the future.

I pleaded with him to talk and to tell me what was wrong. I couldn't understand why he was doing this. He was calm to the point of being almost detached. He had obviously given his decision a lot of thought, unknown to me. He told me that he was sorry and that he knew he was hurting me, but that he wasn't going to change his mind. Although I hate myself for doing it now, I begged him not to go. He packed a holdall and left that night. He said that he would be in touch to

119

arrange getting his stuff and sorting out his share of the bills.

I spent the first few days crying all the time. I called in sick to work and moped about the flat in my pyjamas. I went between feeling very sad to feeling really angry. I comfort ate my way around the clock and hated being in the flat that we once shared and had spent so many happy times in. Everywhere I looked there were reminders of my boyfriend.

Packing all his stuff away was very hard. I thought my heart was going to break. I knew it would be too painful to see him, so we arranged through text messages that he would call one day when I was at work.

I went back to work but found it hard to concentrate. I was living with a permanent black cloud over me. I was full of self-doubt and I felt almost worthless. I felt as if I had been rejected for not being good enough and it hurt. It also hurt when I found out some weeks later that my boyfriend was seen with another woman. My self-esteem plummeted to rock-bottom.

My concentration at work was so low; I pretended to sprain my ankle to get time off. I just couldn't face it anymore. I withdrew totally and I stopped going out with my friends. I was tired all the time and felt so hopeless. I didn't really talk to anyone about how I was feeling. It was bad enough that I felt this way without everyone knowing about it. I was having difficulty sleeping and as a result became very irritable with those around me.

These feelings didn't lift and I had no choice but to go back to work feeling as bad as ever. My weight shot up as I sought comfort from food. I was too embarrassed to tell anyone, so I hid it. The last thing I wanted was everyone staring at me or talking about me. The rumours had started about the weight I was putting on and the last thing that I wanted people to know was the reason for it.

This went on for well over a month and it was draining me. Some of the time I felt there was something wrong with me for feeling as I did; other times I just felt like I was a complete failure. I couldn't shake the dark cloud that continued to hang over me.

I didn't know what to do, to be honest. I didn't think I was ill and didn't know how I would explain it to my doctor. I felt as if I was the only person in the world who felt this way. After about two months it got to the stage where everything in my life was being affected by how I felt and I knew I had to do something. I was taking a lot of sick days and I knew it was only a matter of time before something was said about it. I could not afford to lose my job. I had worked my way up over the years and normally loved my job.

It was the fear of losing my job, rather than finding out what was wrong with me, that helped me make the decision to see my doctor. Even then I *didn't realise I was depressed as such; I just knew that I was going around in a state of constant despair. Even now I can't really explain it, but I struggled to see things clearly and felt that I was a failure all the time.*

My doctor couldn't have been more reassuring. In fact, it was he who told me what my symptoms were before I could tell him. He was spot on. He listed everything I was feeling and explained that they were all normal reactions to a traumatic life-event. I was so relieved because I had convinced myself there was something wrong with me because I couldn't cope.

He explained what depression was and reassured me it was common and it was perfectly normal. He said that sometimes depression needed a helping hand to go away. He listed all the treatments and we discussed which were best for me. He said that, in coming to him, I had already taken the biggest step. I felt as if a huge weight had been lifted from my shoulders.

He prescribed anti-depressants for me and said I would start noticing a change in myself in a couple of weeks. I was concerned about taking tablets in case I got addicted to them or they stopped me from feeling better on my own. He explained that they were not addictive or habit-forming and that they would simply help me to get back to myself. He said we were talking months rather than years. He also made an appointment for me to talk to a psychologist. I wasn't too sure about this at first, but said that I would give it a go.

Although I was still feeling very low in myself, I left the surgery that day feeling that someone finally understood how I felt and was going to help me to get back to myself. For the first time in a couple of months I felt that an end could be in sight and that there was nothing abnormally wrong with me.

Later that week I plucked up the courage to tell a close friend about what I had been going through. Unbelievably, she had gone through something similar some years previously and, like me, had told no one. She had experienced all the same things as me and her reasons for hiding it were the very same as mine. We both felt ashamed, we both felt isolated and we were both afraid of being labelled if we said anything.

It was great talking to each other and I think the chat we had that night really helped both of us. Once I knew I was depressed I wanted to learn everything I could about it. I found Aware's website extremely informative; it answered most of the questions I had and it was really easy to understand. Better still, it treated depression as perfectly normal. Believe me, when you seriously question your own sanity, this was a really big relief.

My psychologist was brilliant. I was a bit dubious about seeing one at first, but after my first session I realised my fears were unfounded. It was a really informal meeting. I had expected some austere person in a white coat; instead I saw a woman in casual clothes in an office that was more like a sitting room than an office. She immediately made me feel comfortable and much of the first meeting was spent talking about my life and my job. I saw her once a week for ten weeks and never once did she ask intrusive questions or make me feel uncomfortable. By our last meeting she had helped me to realise that I was a stronger person than I had given myself credit for and also that what had happened was more a reflection on my ex-boyfriend than it was on me.

Within a few weeks of taking anti-depressants and seeing the psychologist I started to feel better. It really helped to talk to someone who had seen lots of depressed people and I knew that when she told me it was normal, she wasn't just saying it to make me feel better. I was able to ask her anything and not worry about what she thought of me. I know that what happened me can happen anyone and this has helped greatly. It took about three months for me to feel back to myself and I haven't looked back. On my doctor's advice, I continued taking the anti-depressants for six months after I felt as if I didn't need them anymore.

Today, it is nearly two years since my depression. I no longer take anti-depressants. They did their job and my doctor was right; they were not addictive. I have moved flat – I would never have been really able to move on if I continued living there with the skeletons of my past.

I am happier than I have ever been and life is good. I recently got a promotion in work and am now in a new relationship. It's early days, but we are both happy. He has also been hurt, so understands what it's like.

I can only speak for myself, but I feel that a lot more has to be done in order for people to learn about depression. The fear that people have about being labelled is dangerous and wrong. Nobody should feel they have to hide away and not talk about feeling depressed. By doing this, I think it turns depression into something it is not and also stops people from getting help.

I had heard about depression long before I got depressed. However, it wasn't until I was depressed that I understood what it meant. To me it was something that happened to "other" people and usually only after something major had happened, such as the death of somebody close or things like that. I never really thought about it very much and there was nothing that highlighted it or made me think about it on television or anywhere else.

I used to think it would be easy to spot someone who was depressed. I now know that, like me, people often hide it or cover it up. I think depression should be brought out into the open and treated like anything else that makes a person unwell. Depression can be a little tricky, because there is nothing to show you are unwell. For instance, if you have the 'flu, chances are

125

you will have a runny nose. The symptoms of depression are different in that they are not always obvious and some of them can be easily covered up.

I don't worry about depression returning; I am now quite philosophical about it. I am sure I will face some very tough things in the future, but at least I know now that if I do happen to get depressed again, I won't beat myself up over it. I have learned that depression is normal. It is a normal reaction to things that happen in our lives and although we may not be aware of it, many of our friends and family have been through it too. However, the one thing that I still wouldn't do is tell people about it, or speak about it openly. I don't think very much will change until people understand it and this won't happen until there is a greater awareness of it.

◄○►

Getting Help

There are many ways of getting help if you are depressed; however, usually the best place to start is by paying a visit to your doctor. Not only will he or she be familiar with the symptoms of depression, but they will also be able to establish if there is any physical illness that may be causing your depression. Additionally, your doctor will be able to explain all the various treatment options that are available to you.

If you really feel you are unable to talk about how you are feeling with anyone you know, there are Helplines operated by The Samaritans and by Aware. The Samaritans operate on a twenty-four-hour basis and with both Helplines you can talk on a completely anonymous basis to someone who understands. The telephone numbers for both of these organisations are at the back of this book. With depression, you shouldn't feel uncomfortable about asking for help when you need it. You wouldn't hesitate getting help to mend a broken leg; depression is no different. There are certain things you can do to speed your recovery. These include:

- *Acceptance*. The more honest you are, the faster your recovery will be. Denial is a very common reaction to depression. Often people leave it until depression has taken such a hold that it is affecting their ability to cope with everyday things and function normally. Admitting you have a problem is the first, and sometimes the biggest, step on the road to recovery.

- *Be forthcoming*. By giving your doctor the full picture of how you are feeling and acting, it makes it easier to assess the situation and decide on a treatment plan. Sometimes it can be helpful to make notes before you see your doctor; this helps you to remember to mention or ask about something that may concern you.

- *Be comfortable*. There is little to be gained by trying to talk to someone you feel uncomfortable

127

with. There is nothing wrong with seeking a second opinion or looking around for a doctor you feel comfortable with. The same applies to counsellors, psychotherapists and psychiatrists. If cognitive therapy is to be beneficial, you have to trust and feel comfortable with your therapist or doctor.

- *Be patient.* It's very easy to give up on treatment when it doesn't work immediately, or when you don't start feeling better at once. It can take a few weeks for many of the newer SSRI anti-depressants to kick in. I broke two cardinal rules in this regard; the first time I was prescribed them I stopped taking them after a fortnight because I didn't think they were doing anything. On another occasion, after I had been taking them for a while, I stopped suddenly, which was a bad decision given the side effects I experienced. You should never stop taking medication suddenly, because of the risk of side effects. If you are planning to stop taking medication, talk it over with your GP, who will advise on how best to do this, most commonly by gradually reducing the dosage. Equally, although it may appear not to make much sense, medical advice says that you should continue taking anti-depressants for at least six months after you feel back to yourself. The reason for this is to prevent a relapse or recurrence and is important for your long-term recovery.

- *Seek help*. There are a number of things you can do to lessen your chances of getting depression or a recurrence of a depressive episode. Equally, there are things you can do when you are depressed to speed your recovery. Speaking from personal experience, the single most important thing you can do if you feel you may be depressed is to ask for help. Depression doesn't disappear overnight and the longer you avoid asking for help, the worse it gets. The unmanageable doesn't become manageable; it just becomes more unmanageable. Nobody wakes up one morning and decides to be depressed. However, you can wake up depressed one morning and decide to do something about it.

Don't Forget the Children

It is sometimes easy to forget the children (and teenagers) of a depressed parent, who are probably bewildered by what has happened to their previously well parent. Unless they are constantly reassured, children often blame themselves for their parent's illness and feel guilty. Children need to understand that depression is not their fault and, like adults, they cannot fix it with love alone.

Living with a depressed person can be very stressful for a child. Not only are they missing out on the love of the depressed parent, they are also missing out on time with the non-depressed parent, who has to take on the work and responsibilities of their depressed partner. It can be difficult for children, especially younger ones, to understand why their parent cannot interact with them as before. As depression often causes a person to act differently, it is common for a depressed parent to do or say things that are hurtful, which can be very upsetting for the child. Additionally, the symptom of sadness in a depressed person sometimes changes to irritability when it comes to interacting with their children. Conversely, the parent may cry in front of them, which can be very confusing.

Often children feel abandoned and frightened, not only because one of their parents is ill, but also because, to them, if it can happen to one parent, then it could happen to the other. It is generally accepted that it is better to talk about the depression and answer any questions the children may have, rather than try to protect them from it and not speak about it. It is impossible to shield a child completely from the fact that a parent is depressed. By very virtue of the illness, the parent has likely withdrawn from family life, has become uncommunicative and is apathetic.

Additionally, depression often causes notable changes in a person's behaviour and sometimes appearance, which cannot be hidden and which a child will immediately be aware of. You cannot pretend nothing is wrong when a child can see quite clearly that *something* is. It is important to reassure the child that depression is treatable and that people do get better; it just takes time. A good tip in some instances is to liken the illness to another they may be more familiar with, such as heart disease or diabetes.

Rachel's Story

Rachel (16) shares what it was like to live with her depressed parent.

Depression is the one thing I would never wish upon anyone. It not only affects the person suffering but also the loved ones of that person. I was one of those loved ones. I would have to say that living with such an illness was one of the hardest things ever. I know I am young and I know it might sound crazy that I have had such experience for my young age of sixteen; but I truly have.

My mother suffered from depression for about six years, because I can remember it getting really bad and wondering to myself, "What on earth is up with her today?" Even though I wasn't mature enough to understand what it was, it was still there. She tried to cover it up, but I could see that something wasn't right.

When I started secondary school, I have memories of my mother being "spaced out of it" on tranquillisers. I used to think to myself, "Not again." As I got older I wondered why she didn't stop worrying about her pride and get help. It wasn't until I was even older that I realised it wasn't her pride that was stopping her; it was her fear of people pointing at her and saying that she was "one of those". I used to think she was feeling sorry for herself; I couldn't have been more wrong. It hurt so much when I couldn't trust her when she became addicted to tranquillisers. I would never know when she was going to be her "normal" and happy self. It became a rare treat for her to be like this.

She wasn't there for me, which ate away at me and made our relationship almost impossible. I was so angry with her. It's back to normal now, but she missed some really important things when she was sick. Things like my first day of second year and my first day of third year, when she was too sick to come out. She also missed a parent–teacher meeting and a school play I was in that was important to me. I had spent a lot of time practising my part and I really wanted her there. Two hours before it was due to start, I knew she was too sick to come. She looked a mess and hadn't been up out of bed for a few days. When I told her she couldn't be there because she was too "out of it", she said some very hurtful things to me, which still hurt so much I cannot put them into words now. A part of her depression was passed on to my family and me and I do not know what I would have done without my best friends and the rest of my family.

I don't think that people realise how much people with depression need a helping hand and somebody to talk to – not even for advice, but just to listen. My mum pushed me away when I tried to help, but I didn't know how hard it was for her to do even little things. I was oblivious to this and used to say things like, "Just do it" or "It's not that hard" when, in fact, it was a mountain for her to climb.

There are so many things that I only now realise about depression. My mum was too ashamed to talk about it and she never really opened up about it or discussed it with me. Now I understand that she was struggling to come to terms with it in her head just like I was trying to come to terms with it and understand it in my head. For years it seemed like a never-ending circle with no solution. However, my mum finally plucked up the courage to go for help and even though it took a few months before she started acting normally again, it proved that, even though I thought it was hopeless and that she was never going to get better, I was wrong. I think my mum was really brave to say she was sick and to get help. Even though other people told me at the time, I now know that even though sometimes it didn't seem like it, she never stopped loving me for a single minute during her illness. Now if I have any questions I ask my mum and she answers them and I think I will now be able to spot if any of my friends are depressed and be able to help them.

◄○►

Depending on the severity of the depression, those who look after or live with the child or children of a depressed parent should try to get the affected parent to talk with the child about their illness and to offer reassurance that it is not the child's fault. Alternatively, if this is not an option, ensure the child has someone they trust available for them to talk to and to answer their questions or allay their fears. It is important not only to speak in a way that is appropriate to the child's age, but also to be honest with them. For example, a common worry for the child of a depressed parent is that they might get depression. Smaller children may worry if they can "catch it". It is helpful, whether they are vocal about this or not, that it is explained that depression is not contagious like a cold and that you won't get depression from being with somebody who has it.

One thing children young and old will wonder about is death and specifically whether or not their parent is going to die from this illness. This can be discussed in a manner appropriate to age.

Support is vital to children of depressed parents and it doesn't particularly matter where this attention comes from once they have it. Whether a parent, friend or relative, all have the ability to minimise the impact of a depressed person on a child by simply making them feel special and wanted. It helps to encourage children to talk about their feelings and to offer to do things with them that they may be missing out on, such as trips to the cinema, to the park, etc. Older children should be encouraged to maintain their routines and to go out with friends regularly. Children (and teenagers) automatically feel more secure when they see that a situation is under control and they have an adult they can turn to for help. Children (and teenagers) often blame themselves for their parent's illness. They need to hear certain things to help them understand the situation. This can be done by frequently telling the child:

- Your parent's depression is not your fault
- You are not responsible for taking care of your parent's depression
- You are not alone, so many people care about you
- It is okay to feel angry; sad; guilty; afraid, etc.
- Your mother/father still loves you very much
- Your mother/father cannot help how she/he is feeling or acting
- Your mother/father will get better
- I am here if you need to talk
- I think I can understand how you may be feeling

CAMH is Canada's leading addiction and mental health teaching hospital. I would like to thank Phil DiRosa for his assistance and for kind permission to use the following guide, which should help parents, guardians, relatives or teachers to answer most questions children have about depression.

When a parent is depressed . . .
What kids want to know

Children have a lot of questions when someone in their family is sick. When the problem is about depression, it often becomes a secret that nobody talks about. When children don't have answers to their questions, they tend to come up with their own, which may be incorrect and scary! Every parent and child's "beginning conversation" about depression will be different depending on the child's age and ability to manage the information. You know your children best.

This information will help prepare you (whether you are the well parent, the parent with depression, a grandparent or another adult in the child's life) to take the first step. If you have already started talking to a child about depression, this information will give you details to keep the conversation going. It lists common questions children have about their parent's depression, as well as suggestions for how to answer their questions.

Questions Kids Have

What is depression? How does depression work?

- Depression is a disorder that affects how a person feels, thinks and acts.

- When people are depressed, their brain works differently from when they don't have a depression. Our brains help us to think, feel and act in certain ways. Therefore, when people are depressed, they think, feel and act differently from how they do when they're well.

- Depression is not a weakness.

- Depression is a fairly common disorder, even though people don't always talk about it.

Why does my Dad act the way he does? How does it feel to be depressed? What goes on in my Mom's head when she is not herself?

- Depression causes people to act in ways that are different from how they act normally.

- It can be very hard living with a parent who is depressed because that person may do or say things that make children feel bad or confused.

- Most children notice that a parent who is depressed is not as available to do things with them, like playing, talking or driving them places.

- Depression causes many people to be impatient, to be more irritable, and to get angrier than normal. It can also cause someone to feel sad and cry a lot. These reactions from a parent can be very hard on children.

- A person with depression may get tired more easily and spend a lot of time in bed.

- Sometimes people who are depressed have trouble concentrating.

- People with depression may worry a lot more than normal.

- Sometimes people who are depressed have a negative attitude about life, or have low self-confidence.

- Depression can affect people in many different ways. (This would be an opportunity for the parent to discuss his or her own symptoms with the child.)

- As the depression lifts, the person slowly starts acting more like him- or herself again.

What causes depression? How does it start?

- Depression is a disorder, much like diabetes or high blood pressure (hypertension).

- There are many possible causes of depression. Sometimes the causes are not always known. What causes depression in one person can be different from what causes it in another. In some cases, symptoms can appear suddenly for no known reason. In other cases, the symptoms seem to come after a life crisis, stress or other illness.

- It is unclear why, but some people become depressed more easily than others.

- The child is not the cause of the parent's depression.

Will the depression ever be fixed?

- The good news is that depression is very treatable. Seventy-five to eighty-five per cent of adults treated for depression get better.

- Sometimes the depression comes back and it can be treated again.

How can my Mom or Dad get better?

- Many different treatments are available, including medicine and talk therapy.

- Medicine helps to make the chemicals in the brain work better, and that can help the person who is depressed think, feel and behave more normally.

- Talk therapy gets people who are depressed to talk with a therapist about what they are experiencing. The therapy helps them learn new ways to cope and to think, feel, and behave in more positive ways.

Is there anything I can do to make Mom or Dad better?

- Support from family is really important to people with depression, but it is the adults (e.g. doctors and therapists) who are responsible for treating depression, not the kids.

- Even though you can't fix the depression, sometimes just knowing what your parent is going through, and understanding that he or she has a disorder and will get better, can help your parent.

Will it happen to me? Will I get it too?

- No one can ever know for sure if they will get depression at some point in their lives.

- It is natural to worry about this. Just like other illnesses (e.g. arthritis or diabetes), having depression in your family might put you at an increased risk, but then again, it might not. We don't really know.

- It's most important to focus on what you can do to help yourself deal with stress and lead a balanced life.

139

Is there anything I can do so I don't get depression?

- One of the most important things that kids can do to protect against getting depressed is to be open about how they're feeling. It's healthy to let parents or other grown-ups in their life know what they're going through.

- By opening up to parents and other grown-ups who care, kids can get the help they need to feel better and solve problems in their lives.

- Some kids who have a parent with depression don't always talk about the times when they are feeling angry, sad, scared or confused. They think that maybe their parents or other grown-ups don't want to hear about those feelings. However, that's just not true!

- Participating in sports, hobbies and other activities with healthy grown-ups and kids is important because it helps to have fun and feel good about you.

Can parents give it to other people? Is it like a cold? Can you catch depression?

No. Depression isn't like a cold. There is no germ. It's not contagious. There is no way of catching it. Therefore, you can hang out with someone who is depressed without ever having to worry about catching it.

Questions About Self-harm

These questions touch on major issues of interest to children. However, children can ask many different questions about family situations. Once a conversation starts, it is difficult to know exactly what children might ask. Most parents are able to manage "spin-off" questions (e.g. Why is Mom in the hospital? When is Dad coming home?).

The topic of suicide is harder to handle

Many people with depression do not have suicidal thoughts. This is why this material is not included in the question and answer format. If questions arise around suicide or a parent self-harming, here are some ideas on how to share information with children.

When children hear that someone is ill, they naturally wonder if that person might die. Children sometimes ask if depression can kill a person.

While suicide is a risk with depression, it is only one of the many symptoms a person might have. Children should understand that depression does not cause the body to stop working, like a heart attack might – so no, it doesn't kill people. But there are times when people with depression might feel so bad that they say things like "I want to die." This can only be a scary thing for a child to hear. Moreover, once in a while, some people with depression do try to hurt or kill themselves when they think and feel this way.

If discussing this issue with children, it is important to reassure them that:

- The parent has never wanted to hurt or kill him- or herself. (Say this only if true.)

- If the parent were feeling so bad that he or she wanted to die, a doctor, therapist or other adult would help the parent to stop feeling that way.

ABC of Depression

Accept you are ill

Believe you will get through this

Calm thoughts are important and beneficial

Drugs and alcohol should be avoided; they only mask the problem and make it worse

Eat properly – it's easy to become malnourished and lose weight when depressed

Family and friends want to help; try not to shut them out

Give yourself goals and things to look forward to

Hiding away only increases the sense of isolation

Identify the things that cause you stress and look at ways of eliminating them

Jitters and anxiety are common and can be controlled with treatment

Keep active – walk, swim, run – even though you may not feel like it

Look at ways of improving your lifestyle and reducing your workload

Make time to do something you enjoy at least once

Nothing is so bad it cannot be overcome

One day at a time is better than trying to run before you walk

Positive thinking helps to put things into perspective

Quit beating yourself up about things; you are not at fault for being ill

Relaxation techniques may help: massage, yoga and aromatherapy

Sleep patterns may be affected; exercise will help to tire you out

Talk about how you are feeling to someone you trust

Understand what depression is by reading and learning about it

Vegetables and fruit will provide essential vitamins

Weight gain and weight loss are common, a balanced diet is important

You are not alone, despite what you may be feeling

Zero tolerance when it comes to stigma; which is perpetuated by ignorance

Finally, depression is not something people choose to have. However, and this will not become apparent until you emerge the other side of it, depression can be an invaluable life-experience. It is something to learn from, to take strength from, and to emerge from as a stronger and perhaps more insightful person.

143

When I'm Hurting

It's easier for you to walk away, than it is for you to reach out to me.

It's easier for you to look away, than it is for you to see the depth of my despair.

It's easier for you to look through me, than it is for you to see "me".

It's easier for you to distance yourself, than it is for you to really care.

It's easier for you to hear, than it is for you to listen.

It's easier for you to judge, than it is for you to understand.

It's easier for you to label, than it is to get acquainted.

It's easier for you to bask in your joy, than it is for you to feel my pain.

It's easier for you to bewilder at my mysteries, than it is for you to probe deeply into the depths of my soul.

It's easier for me to look away, than it is to let you see the feelings betrayed through my eyes.

It's easier for me to cry, than it is for me to talk.

It's easier for me to walk alone, than it is to risk rejection.

It's easier for me to push you away, than it is for me to be held.

It's easier for me to distance myself, than it is to trust that you won't hurt me.

It's easier for me to die, than it is for me to face life's challenges.

It's hard for me to smile when I am hurting.

It's hard for me to talk when you won't understand.

It's hard for me to reach out when I need help the most.

If only you'd really look at me and see who I am.

If only you cared enough to reach out when I push you away.

If only you'd hold me, without asking why.

If only you'd acknowledge the validity of my feelings.

But it's the easy roads that are most often taken.
And so I hurt alone.

© *Jo A. Witt, USA*

Karina Colgan

What Do You See?

When you look at me, what do you see?
The quiet, outer strength, or the hidden, inner
weakness?

When you look in my eyes, what do you see?
The hard look of resolve, or the tears threatening
to betray my emotions?

Do you see the numb acceptance?
Or the bitter rejection that it can't be different?

My head says, "Leave me alone . . . I can take this."
My heart is pleading, "Don't listen to my head."

It's easier to not have friends,
. . . But that doesn't make it any less lonely.

Does my wall of security keep you out?
Or do you see the hidden door I've made, if one
might only search for it?

I search your eyes in hope that I might find a
secret knowing in them,
But again, I must wait for another day.
And again, I'm left asking aloud in my head . . .
When you look at me, what do you see?

© Lacy Malady, USA

146

3

Depression in Teenagers: A Parent's Guide

"There are two lasting bequests we can give our children. One is roots. The other is wings."

HODDING CARTER JNR.

Depression is the most common emotional problem in adolescence and the greatest risk factor for teenage suicide. In Ireland approximately one in ten of thirteen- to nineteen-year-olds have a depressive disorder, with some professionals experiencing rates as high as 20 per cent in some areas. The highest rates of deliberate self-harm are among females aged fifteen to nineteen years, and suicide is the single biggest killer of young men aged fifteen to twenty-four, taking more lives in this age bracket than road traffic accidents. It is thought that between 30 and 50 per cent of young people who experience a depressive disorder have significant thoughts of suicide and that many young men who die by suicide will have had depressive disorders which were unrecognised or untreated. Sadly, it is estimated that only about 20 per cent of depressed teens will get help.

In one of the largest studies of adolescent mental health ever conducted in Ireland by the National Suicide Research Foundation (NSRF) in 2004, almost 27 per cent of the teenagers surveyed reported experiencing serious personal, emotional, behavioural or mental health problems. The study reported: "findings clearly indicate that there is a 'hidden population' of adolescents with serious mental health problems, who do not come to the attention of healthcare services."

Teenage depression is no different to adult depression insofar as it has the same devastating impact on the teen and, as with adults, it will affect their lives and the lives of their families. It will attack confidence, self-belief and self-worth and will invoke feelings of anger, confusion, despair and self-criticism. Left untreated, it will likely lead to problems at home, at school, with friends and, possibly, with the law.

Although teenagers share many of the symptoms of depression with adults, some symptoms tend to manifest themselves differently in teenagers. For example, anger and aggression may replace the more expected symptoms of withdrawal and sadness. One of the key signs of depression in teenagers is chronic irritability, which may be exhibited through grumpiness, hostility or frequent loss of temper.

Sometimes it can be difficult to spot depression in a teenager because many depressed teens don't look or act sad. They often hide their tears and burst into angry confrontations to deflect attention from the substantive issue. In addition to battling hormonal changes, teenagers battle other pressures on an almost daily basis – everything from peer pressure to their voyage of self-discovery. Parent/teenager conflict is, to a point, part-and-parcel of growing up and starting to assert independence. However, this is sometimes what makes it difficult to tell the difference between teenage depression and moodiness.

Some may turn to alcohol or illegal substances in the hope of feeling better. However, it is also worth noting that some teenagers only become depressed *after* they start abusing these things. Generally, any sustained difference in moods or behaviour should ring warning bells. Parents need to be vigilant about signs and symptoms because most teenagers are unlikely to look for help of their own accord.

<o>

Jenny's Story

Marie and her husband Jim found themselves unexpectedly dealing with depression in their fourteen-year-old daughter.

Jenny was always a bright, happy, bubbly child. She had lots of friends, loved to sing and dance, and meticulously followed whatever fashion was in. Jenny was a much-wanted and long-awaited only child and we showered her with love. She and her dog were inseparable and went everywhere together; you'd rarely see one without the other. When my husband was offered a promotion we had to move house. Jenny was very excited about it and talked about it non-stop. She started packing well in advance of the move and on the day of the move was up at the crack of dawn. We moved at the end of the summer, just before Jenny returned to school.

Things quickly settled down and we got into a new routine. The new house was about a thirty-minute bus journey away from our old house, which meant visiting friends or friends visiting was limited to weekends. After a few weeks Jenny began saying that she missed her friends. Over the next couple of weeks I noticed that she was unusually quiet. She would come in from school, mumble a few words and just go straight up to her room. This continued until the mid-term holidays and once Jenny could visit her friends and they could visit her, she returned to her usual self. However, the real problems started when it was time for Jenny to return to school after the holidays.

She began making every excuse under the sun not to go to school: she had a sore stomach; a sore foot; a headache; a toothache. It became a battle to get her to go to school. I constantly asked her what was wrong, but each time she would say that nothing was wrong. We started to get notes home from teachers about homework not being done and

Jenny not paying attention in class. Exasperated, one night Jim and I sat her down and asked her to tell us what was wrong. We said we knew something was wrong and that she wasn't to say, "nothing".

She said she hated the new house and wished we had never moved. Then she started to sob. Not little sobs, but huge ones that made her whole body tremble. We had never seen her like this, nor had she ever acted out of character in the way she was doing. We decided to take her to the doctor, not really knowing if she could do anything. Jenny told her that she was fed up and was tired all the time. The doctor probed a little more and then examined her. She diagnosed depression, and recommended Jenny see a psychologist, which shocked us a lot. I always thought only adults got depressed, not children.

The doctor said it could take months to get an appointment if we went public, and suggested we went privately rather than waiting, given the state Jenny was in. We agreed and she referred us to one. I have to say, the psychologist was lovely, but she didn't come cheap. It cost us well over €100 the first time, and then €70 every time after that. It was a lot of money to have to find all of a sudden.

The public appointment we received was three months down the line and we knew there was no way we could wait this long to have Jenny treated, so we continued to have her seen privately. It was difficult, but we had no choice because the waiting lists were so long.

Thankfully, counselling worked for Jenny and she was taught how to look positively at the things she thought negatively about. She still misses the old house, but she has made new friends here and can deal with it a lot better now.

—◁◦▷—

One of the greatest challenges parents or guardians face is being able to recognise the symptoms. Parents tend to assume that the family or the home has caused depression when, in fact, the opposite is true; depression causes these problems within the home and the family. Additionally, parents often add to the stress by blaming themselves for their teen's depression – unless you have subjected your child to abuse of any kind, then it is unlikely. Prompt action is vital if you think your teenager may be depressed. The symptoms won't magically disappear by waiting. Although your teen may deny there is a problem, as with adult depression, denial is a common reaction. Equally, sometimes teenagers are not mature enough to recognise the symptoms of depression.

Signs of Teenage Depression

- Lack of energy
- Changes in eating or sleeping habits
- Poor concentration
- Decline in school, college or job performance
- Behaviour that is out of character
- Risk-taking
- Frequent complaints about physical symptoms such as stomach-ache, headache
- Restlessness/agitation
- A prolonged period of being "down-in-the-dumps"
- Medically unexplained aches and pains
- Lack of interest in activities or going out with friends
- Disproportionately sensitive to criticism
- Eating disorders
- Truancy
- Repeated emotional outbursts, shouting or complaining
- Getting into trouble at school, college or work
- Threats of running away
- Feelings of self-worthlessness
- Self-harming
- Thoughts of death or suicide

The advice from experts is: if your child is displaying some of these symptoms, ask yourself: Is this behaviour new? Is it negatively impacting their ability to function normally at school, at home, with friends, with family? If you can answer "yes" to any of these questions, then it is no harm to seek the advice of your family doctor.

Causes of Teenage Depression

- Death of a loved one or a pet
- Domestic violence
- Sexual, emotional or physical abuse
- Divorce or separation of parents
- An alcoholic parent
- Bullying
- Illness that immobilises or restricts movement
- Moving house
- A personal failure, e.g. not winning a competition, getting a lower grade than expected
- Not living up to someone's expectations
- A parent's depression
- Isolation – a report by the Irish Youth Foundation found that a lack of transport and socialising options led many teenagers to suffer from poor self-esteem, depression, and suicide

Things You Can Do

Inform yourself about depression: The more informed you are about an illness the better equipped you are to deal with it. There are many excellent websites, forums, and discussion rooms on the internet. Equally, there are many websites that are specifically targeted at depressed teenagers. It is often helpful for them to read up on their illness and see that they are not alone.

Seek early medical advice: The earlier you make an appointment for your teenager to see a doctor, the better for them and the better it will be for your family. Early diagnosis and treatment can save many months of turmoil and heartache for all concerned. There are a number of things the doctor will do. These will include a physical examination, quite likely involving blood tests to check for any medical causes for the symptoms your child is presenting with. Additionally, the doctor will also look for any other causes by asking specific questions about the child's symptoms, such as how long they have been present, the impact they are having and whether your child has had any recent traumatic events. The doctor will also want to know about possible alcohol or drug use, lifestyle and other medications the teenager may be taking, including the contraceptive pill.

Talk to your teenager: Although you may be pushed away, ignored or shouted at, gentle persistence is paramount. Under normal circumstances teenagers are notorious for their lack of communication skills with parents, so take this into account when you are asking your child to open up about a tough and very personal situation. Your teenager may have feelings of self-loathing, hopelessness, despair and poor concentration, so take things slowly. Tell your child that you love them unconditionally and that you want to help. Don't be afraid to share your concerns with them, being specific about symptoms you have noticed. Refrain from bombarding them with questions and also avoid getting annoyed by what they are saying. Learn to listen, avoid forcing your opinion onto them and do not be judgemental. Whether or not it makes sense, these feelings are very real for your child and they need to know that they can talk without being judged.

Encourage activities: Often teens sequester themselves away in their rooms using only a computer or music for company. Isolation and solitary activity makes depression worse, so suggest ways that your teenager can get out, such as after-school activities, joining a club, or even taking a family dog for a walk. Exercise boosts serotonin levels in the body and contributes to feeling better.

Be open with the family: You can read much more about living with a depressed person and how to deal with other children in Chapter 7. However, to summarise: "protecting" other family members by not talking about it will serve only to make matters worse and permit the minds of siblings to run riot. Make sure other children are not neglected; it is easy to overlook things if all your focus is on the child with depression. Encourage other children to talk about their fears and any other feelings they may have. As well as looking after your depressed teen, it is also important to look after yourself and other family members.

Treatments for Teenage Depression

Research has shown that one of the most effective treatments for teenage depression is psychotherapy and, in particular, cognitive behavioural therapy (CBT). The same principles are used in the treatment of both adults and adolescents and you can read about this type of therapy in greater detail in Chapter 2. Although research shows that drug treatment can be useful, it strongly advocates that it is used in addition to therapy. Your family doctor can both recommend and refer you to a child psychologist or a psychiatrist. With teenage depression, a psychologist will usually look at not only the child, but also their family, their social group and any other factors that may be contributing to the depression. It is not unusual for family and parent therapy to be suggested as part of your child's treatment.

Karina Colgan

What Should I Do if My Child Talks about Suicide?

The threat of suicide by a teenager should *always* be taken seriously, especially when the teenager is suffering from depression. Teens who are seriously depressed often think, speak, or make "attention-getting" attempts at suicide. One in four teenagers will have suicidal thoughts and suicide is the leading cause of death for teens aged fifteen to nineteen in Ireland. Over 11,000 cases of deliberate self-harm are seen in Irish hospitals every year, with the highest rates of deliberate self-harm being among females aged fifteen to nineteen years. For teens abusing alcohol or drugs, the risk of suicide is even greater. Given these statistics, parents should be on the lookout for signs of suicidal thoughts or behaviour, learn what these are and know what action to take.

Common Signs
- Talk of suicide
- Glamourising suicide
- Comments like, "I have nothing to live for" or "I'd be better off dead"
- Saying goodbye to people as if for the final time
- A sudden change in mood or sudden improvement in outlook and perception
- Giving away belongings
- Risky behaviour that endangers life
- Romanticising dying

- Writing about death, dying or suicide
- Stashing tablets

What to do

Although it may seem a tad obvious, immediately seek professional help. You *cannot* deal with this on your own, nor can you "fix it". Your teenager is severely depressed and needs professional help, which may include medication or even hospitalisation. If your teenager is expressing suicidal thoughts or intent, remove obviously dangerous items from the house such as razor blades, sharp knives, pills (whether prescribed or over the counter) and, if applicable, firearms. You should also look around for stockpiles of pills that may be concealed. Understandably, many parents are afraid to address the issue of suicide with their teens because they are scared of the answers. However, there is no need to panic if your child says they have thought about suicide. Next to getting them immediate professional help, it is also important to tell them that you understand they must be in a great deal of emotional pain; constantly assure them that they won't always feel this way and provide non-judgemental and sympathetic support.

As parents of teenagers will know, living through teenage angst can be trying at the best of times. However, living with a depressed teenager can be difficult, emotionally challenging and downright physical exhausting at times. In addition to being on the receiving end of many of your child's negative emotions, you may also find yourself having to battle to get treatment or take on bureaucracy. At times of high emotion and low energy, it is worth pausing to remember that, like adults, your child didn't choose to be depressed. You have to remember that their behaviour, however trying and irrational, is a symptom of their illness. The road to recovery may be a rocky one with temporary setbacks, but it will end. You can do no more than your best, which comes instinctively to most parents, and your child will thank you for it when they are better.

4

A Teenager's Guide
to Depression

**"Simply put, you believe that things or people
make you unhappy, but this is not accurate.
You make yourself unhappy."**

WAYNE DYER

Depression can be a scary thing if you don't know very much about it. You may have seen things on television or heard about it from friends, but very often, what we hear is not always true. There are a lot of rumours and misunderstandings about depression, which can be confusing and upsetting. This chapter is primarily for twelve- to sixteen-year-olds, but older teens and parents/guardians may want to take a look at it, too.

It's a fact; everyone gets fed up sometimes. Lots of things happen to make us feel this way: a bad day at school, a fight with a friend, disappointing exam results, not getting picked for something, etc. Everyone feels bad about something they did and wish they hadn't. Everyone also grieves, because when someone we love or a pet dies, we are sad, and it's okay to be sad when this happens.

However, when we get sad and feel sad for a long time – and sometimes we may not know what is causing us to feel sad – and we cannot control how we are feeling, then it could be a sign of depression. Depression can affect how you think, how you act, what you feel and how you feel. Unlike feeling low or down-in-the-dumps for a little, depression lasts for weeks and sometimes longer. However, the good news is it doesn't last forever and you won't always feel as bad as you do when you are depressed. There are lots of signs and symptoms of depression, which you can read about a little further on.

I spoke to people in your age group when I was writing this book. Some of them had been depressed about something, some of them knew someone who was or had been depressed and some of them knew nothing at all about depression. It was interesting to hear all their different views about it. Depression can mean different things to different people; something that may really upset one person may not upset another person at all. Sometimes, young people who don't know very much about depression don't understand why someone who is depressed is down-in-the-dumps all the time, why they can't get into a good mood or why they have no interest in going out with friends and doing fun things.

It's Good to Talk

A lot of the time, depression makes a person hide away from people. It is very hard to talk to anyone about it, but that's part of being depressed. Ignoring depression won't make it go away and talking about how you feel is one of the very best things you can do. You may not know this, but talking about things that upset us is actually the mind's natural way of healing itself.

The best person you can talk to is the person you find it easiest to talk to. It might be your mum or dad, an older sister or brother, another relative, your best friend. This person is a person you trust and you know will listen to you. If you don't think you can, or if you don't want to talk to any of these people, then have a chat with your family doctor. Sometimes it can be easier talking to someone who isn't part of your family or a friend. Your doctor has seen lots of depressed people and probably knows people who have been depressed. Doctors are used to all the different ways people feel when they are depressed and they won't mind what you say and nothing you say will shock them. They won't even mind if you cry; they know what depression does to people.

Your doctor can arrange for you to see a psychologist – this person is specially trained to listen and to help people find solutions to solve their problems and to start feeling better about things and about themselves. You can read more about what to expect with counselling a little further on.

Things you need to talk about
Depression can seem like the loneliest place in the world and it can be easy to think that nobody understands how you are feeling. Depression can cause some very strong feelings and

thoughts and may also cause you to behave in a way you wouldn't normally behave, which may be dangerous or bad for your health. You should *always* talk to someone if:

- You have thoughts of not wanting to live, of deliberately hurting yourself
- You are being physically, emotionally or sexually abused
- You are being bullied
- You have thoughts of running away
- You are abusing alcohol or drugs
- You can only think negatively about things
- You feel worthless and no use
- You are having problems dealing with family and friends
- You are having problems at school or keeping up with schoolwork
- You are deliberately doing things that you know are dangerous

Helplines

Helplines are a great way to talk to somebody who understands exactly what you are going through. They will listen to you and, if you want, they will advise you or answer any questions you may have. These guys are specially trained and really know what they are talking about, so whatever advice they give you will be good advice.

These Helplines are confidential, which means they don't know who you are or where you are calling from and anything you say is private. You can talk about anything that is worrying you, how you are feeling, if you are depressed, suicidal or feel like running away. They are also there if you just need to rant or just need someone to talk to. Whatever you say will not shock them and they will never judge you.

- **Teen-Line** is especially for teenagers. It's a free number – 1800 833 634 – and it operates on Wednesday from 3.00 p.m. to 6.00 p.m., Thursday to Saturday 9.00 p.m. to 12.00 midnight and on Sunday from 8.00 p.m. – 11.00 p.m. You can check out the website as well: www.teenline.ie

- **Childline** is for children and young people up to the age of eighteen. It is a free number – 1800 666 666 – and operates twenty-four-hours a day, every day of the year. There is lots of information on its website: www.childline.ie

- **Aware** is for people of all ages. ItsLoCall Helpline – 1890 303 302 – operates Monday–Wednesday 10.00 a.m. – 10.00 p.m., and from Thursday to Sunday 10.00 a.m. – 1.00 a.m. They have lots of really helpful information about depression on their website: www.aware.ie

- **The Samaritans** operate twenty-four hours a day, every day of the year. Its Helpline is 1850 60 90 90 and its website: www.samaritans.ie

Darren Bolger was a typical teenager who loved life. He was very caring, loving and showed empathy to others. Darren made two mistakes in his life. His first mistake was that he didn't talk about how he felt inside. His second mistake was a result of the first; he died by suicide on 6 April 2003 aged sixteen years. After Darren's death his mother, Maureen, was shocked to discover the lack of services available for young people in Ireland who may be contemplating suicide or going through difficult times and need someone to talk to. Teenagers expressed this gap in services to Maureen, saying they felt they were in between, too old for one helpline and too young for another. Maureen decided to put her experience and Darren's death into something positive, hence the foundation of Teen-Line Ireland.

MAUREEN BOLGER

Symptoms of Depression in Young People

Depression has lots of symptoms. Sometimes different people will have different symptoms. However, there are some symptoms and feelings that most people who have depression will experience. Having one or two of these symptoms that last only a day or two is most likely not a sign that you are suffering from depression. However, if you have some, or many, of the symptoms below that last for more than a few days, then you should talk to somebody about how you are feeling.

- A feeling of sadness that doesn't go away
- Feeling down all the time and not being able to cheer up or feel happy
- You can't concentrate very well and your grades may fall with schoolwork
- You may find it hard to sleep
- You feel tired all the time
- You can't seem to be able to make your mind up about anything
- You have no confidence
- You don't really care about what you wear
- You feel as if you are no use
- You may put on or lose weight
- You may feel really sensitive about what people say
- Unexplained aches and pains, such as stomach-aches, headaches, aching limbs
- You may burst into tears easily
- You may think about running away
- You are not interested in the things you used to enjoy, such as hobbies and pursuits
- You feel irritable or cranky and people or things easily annoy you
- You may feel guilty for no reason

- You may feel fidgety or restless
- You prefer to be on your own and isolate yourself from your family or friends
- You feel like you are a worthless person
- You may even feel so bad that you think about hurting yourself or about dying

Some of the Things that Help You to Feel Better

Counselling (or therapy) is a very effective way to help people recover from depression. Generally your doctor will refer you to someone who is specially trained in listening to people and helping them to overcome problems. This can be a counsellor, a psychologist or a psychiatrist. You can talk about anything with these people: you may hate your parents, you may have had a bad experience experimenting with sex or drugs, you may be upset over a row with your best friend, a teacher you think has it in for you. . . in fact, anything; these are just examples. The thing about counselling is you talk to someone who will listen, understand and help you. Your counsellor may give you "homework" to do in between your appointments – for example, keeping a diary of your feelings. Your counsellor will also be able to answer your questions and show you solutions.

Support groups can also be really helpful. Here you meet other people who feel just like you, as well as people who have been there and now feel better. You can discuss things with others in the group – sometimes two (or ten) heads are better than one!

Exercise is a really good way to fight feelings of depression. It is known that exercise releases endorphins into your body – these are the body's natural feel-good chemicals and when they are released through exercise, your mood improves and you feel good!

"It's hard to imagine ever feeling normal again when you are depressed. You can't see a future and you can't think positively. I was depressed for five months and it seemed like five years. I didn't go out with my friends and I lost all interest in sports. I stopped playing rugby and spent most of my time alone in my room when I wasn't at school. I lost interest in my schoolwork and started failing tests. My doctor said a psychologist would help me. At first I didn't want to go because I didn't want to talk about personal stuff to a stranger – but after a while I started looking forward to going. She was great and really helped me to start being positive again. She made me realise that I have a lot to offer and I am a good person. Things do get better and you do start feeling like yourself again."

ROBERT (15)

If Someone You Know is Depressed

Maybe one of your friends is depressed and you want to help them. From reading the chapter so far, you will already know lots of things about depression. You will know how important it is that a depressed person is able to talk about how they feel, even though at first they may not want to. Very often, young people who are depressed turn to friends. Sometimes they just want somebody who will listen to them without offering advice or judging them. When your friend is talking to you there may be tears or anger or complete despair.

Dos and Don'ts

- **Do** tell them that you care and you want to help.

- **Don't** tell them to cheer up or try to make jokes.

- **Do** encourage them to talk about how they are feeling.

- **Don't** interrupt the person.

- **Do** ask them questions such as, "What is making you feel this way?" or "What is the problem?" If you can, give examples of how your friend successfully dealt with problems in the past.

- **Don't** look shocked by anything your friend says – this is not to say you won't be shocked by something they say, particularly if they are talking about suicide. However, if you let them know you are shocked they will clam up and not talk anymore.

- **Do** ask your friend if they have thoughts about suicide if they are making comments about it or talking about ending it all – it's okay to do this; you won't be putting the idea into their mind. What you will be doing is giving them permission to talk about it. If your friend says they want to die, it is important to ask them questions, such as "Have you thought of how to do it?" or "Have you ever hurt yourself?" Your friend's answers will give you an idea of how advanced their plans are or if they are only starting to think about it. Regardless of the answers, you *must immediately* tell somebody about this – your friend's parents, a teacher, your own parents. Your friend may be annoyed you have done this, but you may have saved their life.

- **Don't** trivialise how your friend is feeling, even if you think they are not making sense.

- **Do** tell them that you know depression causes people to think and feel differently. Reassure them that depression is treatable and they will feel better.

- **Don't** be sworn to secrecy, particularly if they have been talking about suicide or ending it all. Tell them that nobody else has to know and ask them to get help – if not for themselves, then to do it for you. Tell them that you are not leaving until they agree to get help; tell them you will go with them if they want you to. If they still refuse, tell somebody immediately – their parents, guardian or your parents. It is vital you act.

171

5

Male Depression

"The lowest ebb is the turn of the tide."

HENRY WADSWORTH LONGFELLOW

Contrary to the often-stereotypical image of depression being something that only affects women, it is an illness that affects both men and women. However, because men are generally perceived as "strong" or "capable", the male ego can, and does, stop men from seeking help. Men need to know that having depression doesn't make them any less of a man. Depression in men is a common illness, which is treatable. Seeking help should be seen as a sign of strength, not a weakness. Early intervention can save months of anguish and with the right treatment most people recover from depression.

Many men become masters of disguise when it comes to depression. They want to hide how they are feeling because they often feel shame and fear. Depression can be even more of a silent battle for men than it can be for women, with far fewer men seeking help and, sadly, far more committing suicide.

Men also have a harder time dealing with the stigma of depression and are often of the opinion that to admit to any kind of emotional distress is taboo. It is common for men to try to hide depression by covering up their feelings using alcohol, drugs, sex, work and other things to hide the real problem. This is never a good idea because it serves only to make the problem worse and makes the man feel even more lonely and self-critical.

Studies show that men are at greater risk of their depression going unrecognised and untreated compared to women. There are many reasons for this. Men are known to put off getting help for health problems, preferring instead to play "brave soldiers". Many men think of themselves as tough, confident and capable, which in turn makes it difficult to accept health problems and, in particular, a mental health problem. Men, in general, don't like to admit that they feel fragile or vulnerable – another reason that they often don't ask for help when they become depressed. Additionally, men worry that depression will negatively impact how they are perceived by family members and friends, as well as within the community and by work colleagues.

Men and women differ in experiences and responses to depression. Where women will focus on emotional factors, men focus on the physical symptoms such as fatigue or weight loss/gain. Women are more likely to acknowledge feelings of despair and self-worthlessness than men, who instead tend to complain about fatigue, irritability, sleep problems and loss of interest in work and hobbies.

Some signs of depression are more common in males, however, and these include anger, aggression, violence and substance abuse. Some men deal with depression by throwing themselves compulsively into their work, in an attempt to hide their depression from themselves, family and friends. However, the effect this has on their home life often produces conflict with their wives or partners and, in the process, makes depression worse. Other men may respond to depression by engaging in reckless behaviour, taking risks and putting themselves in harm's way. Depression is seen as a distinct threat to their masculinity, so they deny they have a problem. It is common for a man to deny he has a problem until something really serious happens as a consequence of his illness, such as a partner walking out, a job loss, or arrest, and they are forced to get treatment.

Depression is also known to affect physical health. It keeps stress continually activated, which is something that may damage vital organs such as the heart. According to one US study, in a given year, men with depression are more than twice as likely as men without depression to die of any cause. It also showed that women with depression also have an increased risk of dying, compared with women without depression, but the difference is not as great as it is in men.

Although most studies show depression to be more prevalent in women than men, and certainly statistics support this, it is worth noting that it is possible that the true extent of the prevalence of male depression could be a lot higher than recorded. There are many reasons for this, but they include:

- Men visit their doctors far less frequently than women do, so there is less opportunity for the doctors to pick up signs of problems.

- Depression is known to be a hugely under-reported illness.

- Men are less likely to be able to deal with the stigma.

- Many men are uncomfortable about talking about their feelings or even admitting them to themselves.

- Men are more likely to see depression as a sign of weakness and subsequently try to deal with it themselves rather than seek help or admit to themselves or others that they have a problem.

- Compared with women, some studies show that men are three times as likely to be dependent on alcohol and twice as likely to be dependent on drugs.

- Men will hide depression longer.

Differences Between Male and Female

Men are more likely to act out their inner turmoil while women are more likely to turn their feelings inward. The following chart from *Male Menopause* by Jed Diamond illustrates these differences. I thank Jed for his kind permission to use it and also for taking the time to answer my questions.

WOMEN	MEN
Blame themselves	Feel others are to blame
Feel sad, apathetic and worthless	Feel angry, irritable and ego-inflated
Feel anxious and scared	Feel suspicious and guarded
Avoid conflicts at all costs	Create conflicts
Always try to be nice	Overtly or covertly hostile
Withdraw when feeling hurt	Attack when feeling hurt
Have trouble with self respect	Demand respect from others
Feel they were born to fail	Feel the world set them up to fail
Slow down and are nervous	Restless and agitated
Chronic procrastinator	Compulsive time keeper
Sleep too much	Sleep too little
Trouble setting boundaries	Need control at all costs
Feel guilty for what they do	Feel ashamed for who they are

WOMEN	MEN
Uncomfortable receiving praise	Frustrated if not praised enough
Find it easy to talk about weaknesses and doubts	Terrified to talk about weaknesses and doubts
Strong fear of success	Strong fear of failure
Need to "blend in" to feel safe	Need to be "top dog" to feel safe
Use food, friends and "love" to self-medicate	Use alcohol, TV, sports and sex to self-medicate
Believe their problems could be solved only if they could be a better (spouse, co-worker, parent, friend)	Believe their problems could be solved only if their (spouse, co-worker, parent, friend) would treat them better
Constantly wonder, "Am I loveable enough?"	Constantly wonder, "Am I being loved enough?"

© Jed Diamond

Jed's Story

Jed Diamond is an international educator, psychotherapist for almost forty years, and author of seven books, including the international bestsellers *Male Menopause* and *Irritable Male Syndrome*.

Jed and his wife Carlin each took depression tests as part of a drug treatment programme involving their son. Carlin scored high on the test while he scored low. As a result, Carlin sought and received help for her depression, while Jed continued to deny there was anything wrong with him.

Years later, in response to Carlin's persistent suggestions that he, too, may be suffering from depression, Jed kept insisting, "I'm not depressed, damn it, leave me alone," citing his score from that depression test as "proof" that he was okay. After all, as he candidly says, "I was a therapist, I'd know if I wasn't okay. I was irritable and angry all the time. However, there were reasons for that. I had a lot of stresses on my job, raising kids was not easy, and my wife was going through menopause and having her own problems. 'Who wouldn't be angry?' I would bellow to anyone who would listen."

Carlin received the brunt of his anger, which she fought to deflect. However, what did she expect? Jed thought. She kept doing all these things that irritated him. If she'd just be nicer, more loving, more interested in sex, everything would be okay. It never occurred to him that his constant anger made it nearly impossible for her to be nicer, more loving, more interested in sex.

"I was worried most of the time," Jed reports. "But wasn't that normal? After all, I had to worry about making enough money to pay the bills. I had to worry about losing my job in an economy where someone else got rich while most of us got poorer and poorer. I worried about the children, grown and gone, but still needing help. I worried about my ageing parents. I worried about the state of the world. I worried about getting old. I worried that I worried so much."

It failed to dawn on Jed that his worry was a symptom of an inner problem, not a response to problems that someone else was causing in his life. It never occurred to him that his irritability, anger and blame were symptoms of a type of depression psychiatry is only beginning to wake up to. "My insistence that I wasn't depressed," he finally acknowledged, "nearly ended my marriage and came close to ending my life.

"Fortunately, I listened to my wife's entreaties that I get help. Too many men die, never realising they are depressed, never recognising they have a treatable illness. If you're one of those men, don't wait as long as I did. Your decision may be a matter of life and death."

(Reproduced with kind permission of Jed Diamond)

◄o►

As a world-renowned expert on the subject of male depression, Jed isn't being over-dramatic when he says seeking help can be a life or death decision. Statistics show that men are three times more likely to take their own lives than women. In an effort to understand the male psyche, and also as a way of informing men on a "man-to-man" basis, I asked Jed some male-centric questions about depression. His answers are not primarily those of a professional; they are those of a man who has suffered from depression and emerged the other side a stronger and more positive individual.

Why were you in denial for so long?

I believe the main reason I was in denial so long is that the statements often given on traditional depression questionnaires such as "I had crying spells", "I felt sad", "I felt fearful", etc. did not seem to apply to me. Since there's no blood test for depression, we are diagnosed based on our answers to questions thought to be associated with depression. I came to recognise my own depression, but the symptoms were different than those many women experience. I developed a research study with subjects from over thirty countries and found that depressed men often have different symptoms than depressed women. For instance, depressed men are more likely than depressed women to endorse the following statements: "I feel emotionally numb and closed down"; "I feel empty inside"; "I have trouble controlling my temper"; "I am easily annoyed and become grumpy"; "I have felt I should cut down on my drinking".

As a man who has experienced depression, what would you say to men who are reluctant to seek help?

No one wants to admit they have a problem, particularly an emotional problem, but I know how much depression sapped my joy and happiness and almost ruined my relationship. Getting help was the best thing I ever did for my own wellbeing and that of my wife and family.

As a man, what were the biggest problems you faced in dealing with depression?

Having been properly diagnosed I was prescribed medications and engaged in psychotherapy. They definitely helped and I felt better. Yet, once I felt better I insisted that I was okay, stopped seeing my doctor, discontinued the medications, and then fell back into denial when the symptoms returned. The hardest thing for me was to accept that I needed to keep taking medications and remain in treatment until I really didn't need them any more. (It took me five years. Now I am off medications and feeling fine.)

Why do you think so many depressed men commit suicide?

The simple answer is that they are not properly diagnosed. If we don't recognise symptoms of irritability, anger and alcohol abuse as signs of depression, many men will not be properly treated and the result is that the suicide rate for men is markedly higher than it is for women of the same age. (In the US the suicide rate for males increases dramatically after age fifty, where for women it stays relatively low throughout their later years.)

Even though you were in denial for a time, what symptoms forced you to realise you were suffering from depression?

I read a quote from Dr Kay Redfield Jamison, a psychiatry professor at Johns Hopkins University Medical School. In her book *An Unquiet Mind*, she acknowledged her own battle with mood disorders. The following quote hit me in the gut. It accurately captured what I was feeling. It helped me understand that what I had was depression and her example encouraged me to seek help: "You're irritable and paranoid and humourless and lifeless and critical and demanding, and no reassurance is ever enough. You're frightened and you're frightening, and 'you're not at all like yourself but will be soon', but you know you won't."

What role did your wife and family have?

My wife was great in her consistent and loving support for me. She never blamed me for my bad moods and ill temper. Nor would she allow me to blame her. She quietly but continually suggested that I seek professional help. It took a long while, but I finally listened to her.

How did your depression affect your family?

It very nearly destroyed my marriage.

Looking back, is there anything you know now that you wish you had known then?

I wish I had known how effective treatment could be. Even being a healthcare professional, I resisted the notion that I had a problem. If I did have a problem, I thought I should take care of it myself. If I did need help, I expected I could get it taken care of quickly and easily. I now know that treatment is not simple, fast or easy, but the result is having a life worth living.

What lessons did depression teach you?

It has taught me to be patient with myself and with others. It has shown me how vulnerable we all are and how easy it is to "lose it" when we are under stress and pressure. It has taught me to reach out to others, even when I feel I don't need it or can handle my problems myself.

Why, in developed and progressive countries, do you think stigma remains such a problem in relation to depression?

In countries where being in control is given high value, depression and other mood disorders are stigmatised. Men, even more than women, often are viewed by themselves as less than manly if they acknowledge having a "mental illness".

‹○›

Common Symptoms of Male Depression

Although many of the symptoms of depression affect both men and women *(see Chapter 2)*, these are the most common symptoms for males:

- Feeling low and/or unhappy
- Anger and frustration
- Risk taking – such as dangerous driving, risky sex or extra-marital affairs
- Denial
- Feelings of anxiety
- Low energy/fatigue
- Poor concentration
- Feeling worthless and/or hopeless
- Losing interest in activities and/or people
- Social withdrawal
- Weight loss / weight gain
- Sleep disturbance
- Loss of appetite / increased appetite
- Self-criticism
- Loss of sex drive
- Apathy
- Aggression in a previously passive person
- Lapses in personal appearance and personal hygiene
- Thoughts of suicide
- Alcohol and/or substance abuse
- Working around the clock

"What I felt was devastating. I couldn't eat properly; I couldn't sleep properly; I went around in a permanent state of anxiety. I could feel my personality change and I started to act out of character with those close to me and also with work colleagues, to the point where my position at work became questionable, even though I was working all hours to try to keep my mind off how I was feeling. I felt constantly sad and worthless and my interest in things I once loved vanished. No matter what I did, I couldn't shake the constant feeling of doom and gloom. Only when I felt as if I were going mad and could not continue as I was did I eventually go to my GP for help."

SIMON (34)

Causes

There are many causes for depression, but some of the most common causes for males include:

Relationship Difficulties

For married and cohabiting men, studies show that difficulty in a relationship is the most common single problem connected with depression. Arguments make many men feel uncomfortable, so they tend to try to avoid them or difficult discussions wherever possible. However, this burying-your-head-in-the-sand mentality often drives a man's partner to distraction. They constantly try to talk about the problem, while the man refuses to discuss it and withdraws. This vicious circle often destroys relationships.

Separation and Divorce

Of all men, men in this group (along with men over seventy) are the most likely to kill themselves. There are a number of reasons for this. Apart from the male psyche, which views his role as being the provider and head of a family, the process of separation and divorce often means a man has to move out of the family home, has reduced contact with his children and may find himself under financial strain. These stressful events, coupled with the break-up of a relationship, are causes of depression.

Unemployment

After relationship difficulties, unemployment is the next biggest cause of depression in men. Studies show that up to one in seven men who become unemployed will develop a depressive illness within six months – much higher than for the same period with employed men. This isn't altogether surprising, as men place great importance on work and for many it is a measure of their success, their self-worth and their perceived importance. Equally, many depressed men use work as a distraction, or a way of hiding the problem – which is one of the most common symptoms of male depression.

Life after the loss of a job radically changes. Perks once taken for granted, such as a company car and foreign holidays, disappear and there follows a period of adjustment where perhaps roles are reversed as the wife/partner becomes the main breadwinner and the man adopts the role of homemaker. This can be devastating for a man's sense of self-worth and confidence, particularly if it takes him some time to find another job. This sometimes produces a vicious circle, because depression can make it difficult to muster the energy to seek work, which compounds the depression.

New Baby

Although this is a happy event in a couple's lives, the birth of a baby is a life-changing event. It is widely known that some women suffer from "postnatal depression" after the birth of a baby. However, what is less widely known is that approximately one in ten fathers also suffer from psychological problems following the birth of a baby.

Life changes on many fronts at this time for both parents and brings additional responsibility and pressure. However, for many men, it is the first time they have found themselves in the position of having to compete for their partner's attention and having to share their partner's affection. Men also have to contend with a greatly diminished sex life. New mothers are often simply too tired to think about sex very much during the months after giving birth. Sometimes men perceive this as rejection (which it is not). It is just the physical burden of tiredness on the mother's part, which passes.

Sex

This tends to be something of a double-edged sword insofar as depression can cause sexual problems and sexual problems can cause depression. Like all depressed people, men feel less confident about their bodies and their abilities. While some men go off sex completely, it is common for depressed men to have intercourse as often as normal, but not feeling as satisfied as usual. Additionally, it is not uncommon for a few depressed men to have an increased sex drive, usually as a way of trying to make themselves feel better, or to prove their masculinity. Perhaps this is the reason a common symptom of male depression is partaking in risky/casual sex and extra-marital affairs.

Sexual dysfunction, such as impotence (difficulty in getting and/or maintaining an erection) is a common cause of depression. However, this is a condition for which treatment generally proves to be effective. Men should take consolation from the fact that, as depression improves, so too does sexual performance, desire and satisfaction.

Suicide

Research shows that men are three times more likely to commit suicide than women are. In Ireland, suicide is the biggest killer of young men aged fifteen to twenty-four. In England and Wales, depression is responsible for 3,000 suicides every year. Suicide is also common among men who are separated, widowed or divorced, and more likely if someone is a heavy drinker. It is also prevalent in older men over the age of seventy years.

Men tend to use more lethal means in suicide attempts, which partly accounts for their higher rate of suicide. However, other things must also be taken into account, such as their tendency to move from suicidal thoughts to suicidal actions. Research shows that men take an average of just twelve months to go from contemplating suicide to attempting suicide. In contrast, it takes women about forty-two months. Men are also less likely to show warning signs, which means family and professional recognition and intervention is more difficult.

Threats of suicide or suicidal comments should always be taken seriously. Many attempts at deliberate self-harm are simply a cry for help; however, they often signify serious depression and need to be referred for urgent professional help. *(There is more on suicide in Chapter 9)*.

Treatments

Depression is a treatable illness and there are different treatments for different types of depression. Exercise is thought to be effective in both preventing and treating mild depression, while medication and/or psychological treatments are effective for moderate or severe depression. The key to treating depression is to seek help early before the illness takes a firm hold. Too often, men prefer to ignore symptoms in the hope they will disappear. They don't. In fact, they just get worse.

Psychological treatments look at the issues that may be contributing to or causing depression. It is common for psychologists to use varied approaches, such as establishing how things are viewed and looking at new ways to see these things more positively. You can read more about the types of treatment in Chapter 2.

Medications are commonly used to treat severe depression and also when psychological treatments may not be enough. As one of the physiological causes of depression is associated with an imbalance of certain chemicals in the brain, anti-depressants help to return balance to these chemicals. As modern anti-depressants tend to be slow-releasing, it takes a few weeks before their effects become apparent.

Anti-depressants may cause mild and, usually, temporary side effects (sometimes referred to as adverse effects) in some people. Typically, these are annoying, but not serious. A GP will discuss any likely side effects at the time of prescribing and if he doesn't, you should make a point of asking. As men tend not to ask questions, the most common side effects of modern anti-depressants (SSRIs) include:

- Headaches, which normally go away.

- Temporary nausea.

- Insomnia and nervousness may occur initially but usually disappear over time or with a reduction in dose.

- Agitation and/or feeling jittery; if it happens for the *first* time after taking this medication and persists, consult GP.

- Sexual problems; depression can lower libido and impair sexual performance. However, SSRIs may also provoke sexual dysfunction.

These side effects may affect up to 50 per cent of adults who take anti-depressants. Any prolonged side effects should always be discussed with a doctor. Additionally, anti-depressants should never be stopped suddenly or without consulting your doctor.

Further information on things that can be done to help prevent and fight depression can be found in Chapter 2. Additionally, further information and practical advice for those living with a depressed person can be found in Chapter 7.

6

Depression in Older People

"Old age is not a disease – it is strength and survivorship, triumph over all kinds of vicissitudes and disappointments, trails and illnesses."

SAMUEL JOHNSON

Depression is the most common mental illness found in older people and, with anxiety, is the second most common reason for seeing a doctor. It is perfectly normal to feel sad or despondent during times of loss and disappointment. However, with the passage of time, feelings such as these usually pass. When they do not, they are generally good indicators of depression. Older people are especially prone to depression for a number of reasons and adverse life events, including: physical illness and/or loss of health; chronic pain; death of a loved one and/or friends; and social isolation or exclusion. With age, events such as these sadly become far more common for old people. There is a general assumption that old people are able to cope better with death than young people and therefore do not get as depressed about it. However, both old and young people are equally vulnerable when it comes to being alone with few close friends.

Far too often, depression in older people is dismissed as being "normal" and consequently not thought important enough to warrant seeing a doctor about. Other times, depression in older people goes unrecognised, leading to months of despair. Depression usually responds well to treatment and most symptoms disappear, which makes it doubly sad for it to go undetected and untreated.

Many studies suggest that the signs of depression in the elderly are often confused with the effects of other illnesses commonly associated with this age group. However, depression is *not* a normal or indeed a necessary part of the ageing process. There is a widespread belief that these problems are a natural part of the ageing process but this is not the case: only 20 per cent of people over eighty-five, and 5 per cent over sixty-five, have dementia; 10 to 15 per cent of people over sixty-five have depression.

In fact, many older people are, on the whole, happy with their lives despite the challenges of growing old. Ageing has advantages such as wisdom, patience and understanding, not to mention newfound freedom to indulge in activities and past-times, having more time to spend engaging in personal pursuits and perhaps taking up new activities. However, ageing also has its downsides, such as increased risk of medical problems, retirement, memory loss and, perhaps, a decrease in income.

It is only when older people are left totally alone that depression tends to set in and prevents them from enjoying life and sometimes takes a toll on their health as the physical symptoms of depression take hold. Another event that tends to cause depression in older people, particularly after the death of a loved one, is relocating, either by downsizing or by moving into sheltered accommodation or a retirement home. It can be a big wrench to leave behind somewhere one has lived for a long time, with all its memories. Very often their home is a link with the past and with loved ones who have passed on.

While depression is not a normal part of growing older, it is important to accept that older people have more reason to feel sad than younger people do. Loss of mobility, bereavement, increased dependence on others and an increasing inability to do things once taken for granted are all things older people have to contend with over the passage of time. It is important that family members and the medical profession are able to distinguish between depression and normal reactions to loss such as temporary sadness, despondency and lethargy, which should pass.

Irrespective of age or gender, depression should always be viewed as an illness because its symptoms impact a person both mentally and physically. In older people, untreated depression is thought to lead to faster physical and mental decline and even premature death. Research shows that isolation has a dual role in depression, as it is both a cause and a symptom of the illness. Depression is most recognised by persistent sadness and apathy that does not improve over time and impacts a person's normal functions and activities. Depression in older people differs slightly than in younger people insofar as older people are less likely to complain of feeling low, but more likely to complain of physical symptoms such as increased aches and pains. Additionally, some older people who are depressed may experience bouts of confusion and forgetfulness. These symptoms are also indicative of dementia, so it is easy to confuse depression with dementia. Depression will usually be accompanied by other symptoms in addition to confusion and forgetfulness, but all symptoms respond well to treatment and generally disappear.

—◄◦►—

Penny's Story

Penny is sixty-eight years old and suffered with depression for much of her adult life. She finally sought help when her thoughts turned to suicide. She says she hasn't looked back since and now enjoys an active and fulfilling life.

My depression wasn't diagnosed until I was almost sixty and by then I had suffered with it for many years without knowing what it was. Initially it manifested itself in the form of severe anxiety and negativity. As time passed and with no treatment these feelings were joined by feelings of apathy and, eventually, by suicidal thoughts. At my worst I just wanted the feeling of emptiness and worthlessness to end. During my depression I said and did things

I was embarrassed about afterwards, but I never thought that it was because of depression I was doing these things or acting differently. It was like I pressed an invisible self-destruct button.

Everything was an effort and I know my thinking was distorted during depressive episodes, which became constant in the years leading up to me seeking help. My behaviour was increasingly erratic and I turned to alcohol in an effort to block out the black clouds that seemed to hang over me constantly. One drink in the evening quickly turned into two or three and before I knew it I was going through a bottle or two of wine in one sitting. Of course, the alcohol didn't take the problem away and I was trying to cope with hangovers on top of everything else. I was in denial, no question about it. I saw depression as a weakness in my personality. It was only when I finally got treatment that I realised this was not the case. At my lowest point I thought about suicide quite a lot. The thought of escaping the gloom of depression in a painless way was very appealing. It would also have dealt with the fear I had about growing old and losing my dignity and independence.

Therapy taught me to see retirement as an opportunity, not as a negative. It took me many months to believe this for myself, though. I knew I had to get some kind of help when I started thinking about suicide as an answer. Even though I seriously considered it, there was a part of me that rebelled against the idea. Depressed and non-depressed people view suicide differently. Someone who is not suffering from depression views suicide as leaving all the good things in life behind, such as family, friends and the like. A depressed person, however, views it completely differently. They see it as a way of leaving all the bad things behind, which is why I think many depressed people have suicidal thoughts and why so many take their own lives.

I now know depression is an illness that can be effectively treated. I would say to anyone who thinks they may be depressed to seek and accept help. Don't wait until it has crippled you. Life is for living and to waste months or years of your life so needlessly is time you can never get back. I've realised that there are a lot of perks to being older and instead of moping about I have joined so many organisations I barely have a minute to spare. I do quite a bit of volunteer work and this gives me a great sense of purpose and being valued, as well as putting something back into my community. I've recently completed a computer course and although I'll never be a computer buff, I have made internet friends all over the world who share many of my interests and hobbies. My greatest piece of advice is to be proactive and get help. I wish I hadn't wasted so much time in isolation when help was so readily available.

❧

Common Symptoms of Depression in Older People

Depression does not discriminate against age and both young and old people share many of its symptoms. However, there are some symptoms that are more apparent in older people. Additionally, older people often have physical illnesses that can make depression difficult to recognise. For example, symptoms such as constant tiredness, loss of appetite and irritability may present in both physical illness and depression. Older people are also less likely to complain of feeling down, so often it is only by other people recognising the symptoms of depression that treatment is sought.

- Unexplained aches and pains
- Increased anxiety and irritability
- Sustained sadness, not lifted by happy events
- Withdrawal from activities that were previously enjoyed
- Disturbed sleep patterns
- Changes in appetite and/or weight
- Feelings of guilt and self-blame
- Difficulty concentrating or memory problems
- Withdrawal from family and friends
- Decline in personal hygiene and appearance
- Sense of worthlessness and despair

- Pessimism about the future

- Prolonged grief after a bereavement

- Family or prior history of depression

- Despondency

- Talk of death or suicide

Common Causes of Depression in Older People

Although there is no single, definitive answer to the question of cause, many factors – psychological, biological, environmental and genetic – likely contribute to the development of depression. Physical illness is more prevalent in older people and diseases such as strokes and heart attacks frequently cause depression. For many, the onset of old age is a time of great change, which people adapt to with varying degrees of acceptance. Changes in status and position in society, wealth, opportunity, friends and companions may be contributory factors to depression. Sexual dysfunction is also more common in this age group, which often leads to feelings of inadequacy and poor self-esteem (this is treatable). In some cases, depression can be a side effect of medications commonly prescribed to older people, so it is worth mentioning this to your GP if you are feeling low for no apparent reason.

Older women are at greatest risk when it comes to depression. In addition to women being three times more likely than men to suffer from depression, older women also have to contend with hormonal changes, which although easily treated, may make them more susceptible. Women often find themselves in the role of carers, which can also contribute to higher rates of depression. Factors such as being unmarried/widowed or poor social networks contribute to depression in both men and women. Other common causes include:

- Death of spouse or loved one
- Life experiences such as moving house or retirement
- Deterioration in sight/hearing/mobility
- Illness/chronic pain
- Stress
- Loss of status
- Frustration by memory loss
- Poor self-esteem
- Substance abuse
- Increased dependency on others
- Some medications
- Fear of dying and death

Treatments for Depression
in Older People

Older people respond well to treatment for depression. It is generally accepted that around 80 per cent of older adults improve when they receive treatment with anti-depressants, psychotherapy, or a combination of both. Older people with mild depression respond well to a class of drugs called selective serotonin re-uptake inhibitors (SSRIs). These cause fewer side effects and interact less with other medications *(You can read more about these in Chapter 2).*

Non-pharmacological approaches, such as psychotherapy, exercise and social activities, are also known to work well in reducing and sometimes preventing depression from recurring. As Penny advocates in her story, volunteer programmes are a great way of getting involved in the community and regaining a sense of purpose and self-worth. It also stops a person from sitting around moping and stimulates the brain, which is particularly important as you advance in years. Exercise has therapeutic value, as well as being good for health.

Many older people use age as an excuse to stop exercising when, in fact, regular exercise has many definite benefits for older people. Interestingly, much of the body's loss of flexibility that is attributed to ageing is, in fact, caused by inactivity.

Walking is one of the best forms of exercise there is. It costs nothing, can be done at any time and is high in cardiovascular and other health benefits such as decreased risk of depression; improved blood pressure; improved sleep; decreased risk of obesity; improved agility; and decreased risk of diabetes, to name but a few.

Exercise doesn't have to be strenuous or vigorous to be effective. A regular amount of moderate exercise has proven health benefits, e.g. walking for thirty minutes every day. However, if you have been inactive and want to start exercising, get the okay from your doctor first. Start slowly with about ten minutes a day, gradually building up at a pace that is comfortable for you. Minor discomfort is to be expected at first, but it shouldn't hurt. If it hurts, stop and check with your doctor whether you are overdoing it. The maxim, "no pain, no gain" does not apply in this instance!

Like other illnesses, depression is a disease of varying severity and can be successfully treated. However, with depression, once you are well again it is important to stay well. Often this means continuing on medication long after you start feeling well again. The reason for this is to reduce the risk of recurrence. Generally, experts recommend treatment should continue for at least six months after the first occurrence of depression. For those who have suffered from up to three depressive episodes during their life, it is usual to continue treatment for up to two years after the episode passes, and for those who have suffered from more than three episodes of depression, treatment may (but not always) be life-long.

Geriatric Depression Scale

J.A. Yesavage and others first developed this Geriatric Depression Scale (GDS) in 1982 and it is one of the tests commonly used to evaluate depression in older people. Although its efficacy has well-established reliability and validity, diagnosis of depression should not be made on the results of this test alone. A score of over ten certainly indicates depression and warrants a visit to your doctor to discuss how you are feeling. The accuracy of this test depends *entirely* on the honesty of your answers.

Mood Assessment Scale	Yes	No
1. Are you basically satisfied with your life?	☐	☐
2. Have you dropped many of your activities and interests?	☐	☐
3. Do you feel that your life is empty?	☐	☐
4. Do you often get bored?	☐	☐
5. Are you hopeful about the future?	☐	☐
6. Are you bothered by thoughts you can't get out of your head?	☐	☐
7. Are you in good spirits most of the time?	☐	☐

	Yes	No
8. Are you afraid that something bad is going to happen to you?	☐	☐
9. Do you feel happy most of the time?	☐	☐
10. Do you often feel helpless?	☐	☐
11. Do you often get restless and fidgety?	☐	☐
12. Do you prefer to stay at home, rather than going out and doing new things?	☐	☐
13. Do you frequently worry about the future?	☐	☐
14. Do you feel you have more problems with memory than most?	☐	☐
15. Do you think it is wonderful to be alive now?	☐	☐
16. Do you often feel downhearted and blue?	☐	☐
17. Do you feel pretty worthless the way you are now?	☐	☐
18. Do you worry a lot about the past?	☐	☐

	Yes	No
19. Do you find life very exciting?	☐	☐
20. Is it hard for you to get started on new projects?	☐	☐
21. Do you feel full of energy?	☐	☐
22. Do you feel that your situation is hopeless?	☐	☐
23. Do you think that most people are better off than you are?	☐	☐
24. Do you frequently get upset over little things?	☐	☐
25. Do you frequently feel like crying?	☐	☐
26. Do you have trouble concentrating?	☐	☐
27. Do you enjoy getting up in the morning?	☐	☐
28. Do you prefer to avoid social gatherings?	☐	☐
29. Is it easy for you to make decisions?	☐	☐
30. Is your mind as clear as it used to be?	☐	☐

SCORING

This is the original scoring for the scale:
One point for each of these answers.

Cut-off:

normal: 0–9;

mild depressives: 10–19;

severe depressives: 20–30.

1. No	2. Yes	3. Yes	4. Yes	5. No
6. Yes	7. No	8. Yes	9. No	10. Yes
11. Yes	12. Yes	13. Yes	14. Yes	15. No
16. Yes	17. Yes	18. Yes	19. No	20. Yes
21. No	22. Yes	23. Yes	24. Yes	25. Yes
26. Yes	27. No	28. Yes	29. No	30. No

Source: Brink, T.L., Yesavage, J.A., Lum, O., Heersema, P., Adey, M.B., Rose, T.L., *Screening tests for geriatric depression (1982).*

7

Living with a
Depressed Person

**"We cannot change anything unless we accept it.
Condemnation does not liberate, it oppresses."**

CARL JUNG

Whether it's a spouse or another loved one, living with a depressed person is not easy. The misery of depression extends beyond those suffering it to their families and friends, who often have to assume the role of omnipotent partner/parent/friend while sometimes remaining as invisible people in the background, but who may be affected almost as much as the sufferer. It has the potential to cause untold stress to those living with a depressed person unless they are prepared for it and know what to do and how to react to symptoms. It is a natural instinct to want immediately to "make it better", but depression doesn't work like this and there is no magic wand.

The love and support of family members and friends assists greatly in a loved one's recovery; however, unless you take care of your own needs and the needs of other family members, you will find yourself being dragged down and

209

will be of little use to anyone. The better you feel, the more able you are to provide support and encouragement to a depressed loved one.

Depressed people often engender tremendous guilt in those around them and it is common to feel as if nothing you do is of any use. However, feelings of guilt and blame are common and it is vital to know – and also to accept – that a loved one's depression is not your fault and you should not feel responsible for their lack of happiness. It is something you have no control over. There's nothing wrong with you and you have nothing to feel guilty about. You can't relieve or cure depression with love alone, any more than you can cure diabetes with just love. People who are depressed need professional help and/or medication.

A depressed person can be likened to the old adage, "You can bring a horse to water, but you cannot make him drink." You can only do so much; ultimately the decision to seek help is a decision that rests only with the depressed person. Getting a loved one to seek help is very important, but so too is maintaining your own health. Don't be afraid to admit feeling helpless or powerless to do anything; it is normal to feel this way. Depression can be a frightening and overwhelming thing to have to deal with; to see your previously happy and confident partner reduced to an often apathetic and emotional wreck is not an easy thing to deal with.

It is important to know that it is okay to take a step back and seek support from other family members or friends. If things become too much, think about getting counselling for yourself or join a support group. The internet is a great way of connecting with other people who are in exactly the same position and who provide you not only with support and encouragement, but may also be able to offer practical advice. By getting support or by confiding in someone you trust and somebody you know will listen in a non-judgemental way, you create an outlet in which to vent how you are feeling. If you feel as if you are somehow betraying your loved one by talking about the situation to an outsider, remember that by being able to offload your emotions and not having to suppress them, you are in a far better position to deal with theirs.

When a partner is depressed it is common to feel isolated, confused, afraid, angry or unloved. You yearn for the person who was and although you may not be aware of it, you are actually grieving for that person. In addition to not being able to do simple everyday things such as help out with household chores or family responsibilities, a depressed partner is often unable to connect on an emotional level with anybody, which can be understandably hurtful for their partner. The problem can be compounded when the depressed person is a man, who may point-blank refuse to admit he is depressed and needs help, for fear of not being "manly". He may try to conceal the problem with alcohol or by working around the clock, common male reactions to depression. He may also be unwilling or unable to talk about his feelings, instead choosing to isolate himself from you and from the rest of the family.

Next to getting a depressed person to seek help, the most important thing you can do for them is not to make excuses on their behalf or lie for them. If you find yourself doing this, you are not only feeding their denial, you are also delaying them from getting the help they need. Often, getting a depressed person to get help is all that stands between you and your self-preservation. Depressed people often frustrate and alienate those around them. There are few, if any, positives to be gained by being a facilitator. Try not to take it personally – it is not personal; they are ill and they cannot help how they behave.

It is vitally important to prevent yourself from getting sucked into their depression. The additional stress, extra responsibilities and emotional upheaval combine to make you particularly vulnerable. A depressed person may cry a lot – not because they feel particularly sad, but because they feel empty and dead inside. It can be hurtful to a loved one to know that they are not enough to fill this void. It is important to make sure that you continue to have some sort of a social life with your friends, even if it is a reduced one – a regular release is important for you and, if applicable, your children. Also keep an eye on your own health, particularly your diet. Eating properly is important if you are to keep your strength up – a depressed person is not the only person fighting a battle.

Peter's Story

Peter (46) has been married for eighteen years. His wife suffered from depression for eighteen months and during this time it wreaked havoc on their family, their relationship and their finances.

Looking back, my wife's depression was a pretty sudden thing, or at least it seemed that way, I didn't know what was wrong with her. All I knew was that, one day, she wouldn't get out of bed to go to work and I had to ring her office to say she was sick. She didn't get up to get the children off to school and she was still in bed when I got home from work that evening. Her mother was there, doing homework with the children. She had to collect them from school after my wife rang her. This was the start of two years of hell, which saw me almost have a breakdown, as well as my wife. Sometimes people don't realise the effect depression has on the whole family; it's not just one person who suffers.

My wife lost her job as a result of a prolonged absence from work and this hit us very hard financially as we were a two-income family. She got a disability benefit, but this fell far short of what we were used to and we had to readjust our finances

213

and re-mortgage the house just to get by. My wife went from being a fun-loving and bubbly person, into a despondent wreck who refused to acknowledge anything was wrong for months. She wouldn't accept that her condition was getting worse and got abusive when I suggested she seek help. I was resentful of her illness for quite a while. I was running myself ragged trying to work full-time, come home and do the kids' homework with them, get dinner, put them to bed, do the household chores and look after my wife, who never left the bedroom. I was living my life on a knife-edge and walking on eggshells so as not to upset my wife or make her any worse. I don't know whether it was because I am a man, but I never talked about how she was with anyone other than her mother. I felt as if I was somehow to blame and that I should have known what to do to make her better. I know now that it was nothing to do with me. She is an only child, so she had no sisters or brothers I could have enlisted to talk to her. I was too embarrassed to let my family know the true extent of the problem and constantly covered up what was going on or made excuses on her behalf.

I didn't have a minute to myself and had to stop going out with my friends and playing football. It was like being in a prison and I felt very isolated. The kids were very confused and didn't know what was wrong with their mother. The younger one began acting up in school and I had to attend a meeting with his teacher to explain what was happening at home. I felt so embarrassed; I know this sounds bad, but it was how I felt. Eventually, after months of pleading, my wife agreed to see a doctor. We went together and it was only then that I got a glimpse of what she was going through. She was prescribed anti-depressants and although they didn't work straight away, when they did start working the difference was amazing. She also went to counselling, which seemed to help her enormously.

I read up on depression so I could understand as much as I could about the illness. The more I read, the more I could relate to my wife. It took about six months from when she started treatment for her to be pretty much back to herself and her road to recovery wasn't all plain sailing. During her recovery she had some bad days, but thankfully these were few and far between and eventually disappeared altogether. The kids are delighted to have their mother back and I am delighted to have my wife back.

It wasn't until my wife was well on the road to recovery that I confided in my sister about what had been going on. She wasn't shocked, or if she was, she didn't show it. She was just sad that I hadn't confided in her and the rest of my family and allowed them to help the children and me and to have provided much-needed respite.

My wife has now returned to work and our family life is back to how it used to be before her *illness. I think we have both learned a lot from what has happened and we are certainly more conscious of how fragile a person can be without actually knowing they are. These days we don't stress about the little things; they don't matter quite so much anymore.*

--<o>--

Unlike other illnesses where sufferers would go to the ends of the earth for treatment that might make them better, depressed people do not welcome support and, most of the time, they are reluctant to seek help for their illness. This is not so much a conscious decision, as an inability to muster enough energy or interest. To a non-depressed person, it may look as if a depressed person is being lazy, or perhaps exaggerating their illness to avoid doing something. This, however, is not the case. Simple things and even simple thinking and rationalisation are distorted to a person who is depressed. Apathy often prevents them from wanting to seek help because they don't and can't see a future.

The symptoms of depression often combine to make a depressed person's state of mind very hard to penetrate, thus making offers of help difficult or downright ignored. I know that when I was in the depths of depression and staying in bed, nothing – and I mean nothing: not my children; not my family; not my friends – could get through to me. Nothing they said or did changed how I felt for many months. However, their unconditional love and support was of great comfort after I had made the decision to get help and started my journey back to normality. One thing you can do for a depressed person is to listen to them without judging, without forcing your opinion onto them and without dismissing or trivialising what they may have to say. Be sympathetic, even if what they are saying is completely irrational and misguided. Remember, at this time, it makes sense to a depressed person. It's okay to ask them how they feel, or to tell them you don't understand what it is they are trying to say. You may find your patience being tested, but don't give up.

The single best thing you can do if your partner or a loved one is depressed is to read up on depression. Educate yourself as much as possible about the signs, the symptoms and the best and most effective ways to deal with them. It is equally important to distinguish fact from fiction – stigma and myth perpetuate many misunder-standings and inaccuracies about this illness, so inform yourself and know what you can actually expect as distinct to what you may "think" you can expect.

Secondly, however hard it may be at times – and believe me you will be frequently pushed to your limit by your depressed partner – always try to remember that they are ill. They did not choose to be ill and their illness is responsible for how they are acting, not the person you know them to really be. It can be difficult not to get angry or frustrated, but if you do, try not to show it in front of

217

the depressed person. Lastly, although it will be difficult at times, do not take a depressed person's behaviour, actions or words personally.

How to Talk to a Depressed Person

Depression extinguishes hope for the future and propels a person into the depths of despair. It invokes feelings of worthlessness, of helplessness and of apathy. Unless you have personally been there, you cannot begin to empathise with how this feels, nor should you pretend to. The worst thing you can utter to someone who is suffering from depression is a platitude. Although they are often well meaning, platitudes are unhelpful and are to be avoided. "Get over it" is possibly the single worst thing you can say to a person who is suffering from depression. Although often said in an effort to be well-meaning, it is only people who haven't the first clue about the agony you are going through who say something as cruel as this. There is little point getting angry with a depressed person because, although it may not seem like it, they are doing their best to battle the illness, believe me.

Depression is something that attacks your every sense, your very being. It shakes you to the core and shatters your confidence. This often-unexpected illness turns your world upside down, sees you fighting the battle of your life, and you are supposed to simply "get over it"? If it were this simple then depression wouldn't be the epidemic it is today.

Then, of course, there is the flip-side. The half-hearted offerings of help; the easy-way-out cards that are easier than words; the avoidance of personal contact by sending sporadic emails; the insincerity of asking how you are without really listening to your reply, or perhaps more importantly, your *failure* to reply. Then there are the people who really want to help, but are just too busy; between work and kids, they just don't have a minute to spare . . . but hey, that's okay, because they *are* thinking about you, right? Wrong! Ignoring a person doesn't make the problem go away; it serves only to perpetuate the depressed person's feeling of failure and worthlessness.

Depression will touch one in three people in their lifetimes; it is better to understand it than to fear it, and it is better to know what to say and what not to say. Here are some of the most common things you should *not* say and why:

What have you got to be depressed about?

What affects one person may not affect another. Don't judge a depressed person by how you think you would react in their situation.

There are people worse off than you are.

Do you think a depressed person doesn't know this? Of course they do. However, when you are depressed it matters not how many people may or may not be worse off than you.

Loosen up; things could be worse.

A depressed person cannot "loosen up" and, for them, things *are* pretty bad.

You need to get out more.

One of the first things a depressed person does is isolate themselves from family and friends. They do not want to get up, never mind go out.

If you made more of an effort, it might help.

A person doesn't choose to be depressed. Try to imagine walking around in a fog carrying ten-kilo weights; that's what it feels like day in, day out for a depressed person.

Pull yourself together.

Would you tell someone with cancer to get a grip? Depressed people cannot pull themselves together. If they could, they wouldn't be depressed.

What doesn't kill you; makes you stronger.

The last thing a depressed person feels is strong. They are at their most vulnerable and weakest point.

Treat yourself to something nice; it'll cheer you up.

A depressed person cannot cheer up and they have no interest in buying something nice.

This too shall pass.

Unless you have been there, this should never be said. It invalidates depression as an illness.

I know how you feel.

I really doubt it, and unless you have suffered from depression, refrain from saying this as it is patronising.

I can imagine what you must be going through.

> The hell that is depression cannot be imagined; it has to be lived.

Have a nice hot bath; that will make you feel better.

> Climbing Everest would be as likely for someone in the grip of severe depression.

I'll make you something nice to eat.

> A depressed person often has no appetite and no interest in food.

It's all in your head.

> Well, of course it is; that's the problem.

You're making me depressed just looking at you.

> If this is how you feel, stay away from the depressed person because you are doing them no favours by making them feel worse than they already feel.

You're better/stronger than this.

> Depression is an illness, not a weakness, and it's not relieved by an act of will.

Cheer up!

> Nothing matters to a depressed person.

This is what I think . . .

> Don't force your opinion onto a depressed person; they won't hear what you are saying until they are ready to listen. Depressed people often only want someone who will listen without interrupting them.

> **What will people think if they knew you were acting like this?**
>
> A depressed person doesn't care what people think.
>
> **You'll feel better after a night out.**
>
> No, they won't. It could be many months before a depressed person feels up to venturing out. I know some of my own friends couldn't understand why I didn't want to go out for many months.

Conversely, there are constructive things you can say to a depressed people that do manage to penetrate their darkness, even though they may not always acknowledge it at the time. Although your immediate thought will probably be to do with trying to "fix" the problem as soon as possible, realise that acceptance of and recovery from depression takes time. A depressed person will not talk to anyone until they have first accepted to themselves that they need help. Some of the things you should say include:

- *You are not alone.*
- *I am here if you need me.*
- *I am not giving up on you, no matter what you say or do.*
- *You're not mad and you're not going crazy.*

- *I'm not going to pretend I know how you feel, but if you want to talk about it I'm here.*

- *Please tell me if there is anything at all I can do to help.*

- *We will get through this together.*

8

When a Friend is Depressed

"We can't solve problems by using the same kind of thinking we used when we created them."

ALBERT EINSTEIN

It can be difficult to know what to do when a friend is depressed. During my illness my friends acted in different ways: most sent the occasional well-meaning text or email, not really knowing what to say or do and choosing not to comment on my failure to reply. A couple sent almost daily texts and left voicemails even though they never received a response; and one wouldn't accept my social isolation and insisted on speaking to me and calling to see me regardless of what I wanted. Of course, many of the people I knew had no idea what was going on other than that I was making constant excuses not to attend events or go out.

Some experts are of the opinion that social support helps to treat depression and that by constantly reaching out to your depressed friend, you are reinforcing the fact that you care and you are aware of their turmoil. By continuing to include your friend in social occasions – invites to nights out, the cinema, a meal – it means they know that you are thinking of them. The likelihood of getting a response, never mind them actually attending, are very low, so expect nothing in return for your efforts.

I noticed people making the effort and although I didn't have the mental energy to respond, I was grateful that they had. However, I also noticed when some stopped inviting me out, or contacting me, probably because they got fed up with me cancelling at the last minute and then getting no response time, after time, after time. . . If, after a long time, your friend finally makes contact, desist the urge to say something sarcastic like, "Nice to know you are still alive" or "About time, I'd given up on hearing from you". Instead treat the contact as if it's the most natural thing in the world and don't be afraid to ask how they are feeling or say that it is lovely to hear from them. Often it will have taken a lot of courage and strength on your friend's behalf to make contact.

It can be all too easy to send the odd text or email to ease your conscience without giving any great deal of thought to the reasons why you would not get a response. It is all too easy to avoid calling or having personal contact; at times technology has its place, but this is not one of them. True, you may not get to see your friend if you call, but it will be comforting for them to know that you made the effort. Don't sit around waiting for your friend to make contact. A depressed person *cannot* pick up the phone or reply to a text. It's not that they don't want to; they are not able to. Spending time on a depressed friend is unrewarding and it is a thankless job . . . at least until they are on the road to recovery – the thanks will come then.

‹◇›

Laura's Story

Laura (26) helped her friend through depression, but it was quite some time before she realised what was wrong.

It's difficult to know the point at which I realised something was wrong with my friend. I had been trying to get her to come out for a meal for what seemed like ages. She had suddenly stopped coming to Weight Watchers and I was anxious to find out why. It seemed every time I called I got her voicemail and she didn't seem to be getting my emails because I was getting no replies to them. Not being able to get in touch with her began to bug at me, so I phoned her in work one day only to be told that she was off sick.

I think that's when I realised something must be wrong with her. That evening when she didn't answer the phone to me, I sent her a text saying that I was calling to see her. I got a text back from her saying that she was feeling really sick and that she wasn't really up to company. I replied and said I hoped she would soon be feeling better and that I would contact her again in a few days.

Between one thing and another, and my being really busy in work, it went out of my mind. It wasn't until over a week later that I remembered I had told her I would call. I got a pang of guilt, but

227

called her. Again I got no answer and this time my text went unanswered as well. To be honest, at this point I was fed up trying to contact her when she never made any effort to get in touch with me. I was also annoyed that she hadn't told me what was going on and had stopped coming to the slimming class with me without as much as a text.

However, when I still hadn't heard anything a couple of weeks later, I decided to make one last attempt to make contact with her. I phoned her at work, but was told that she was on an extended leave of absence. I got really worried then, so that evening I called to her house unannounced. I rang the bell but there was no answer. I peered through the letterbox and couldn't hear a sound. I was just about to ring the bell again when I heard a faint cough. It sounded muffled, as if she didn't want anyone to hear. I shouted her name through the letterbox and said that if she didn't answer the door I was calling the gardaí. I waited for what seemed like an eternity for her to respond. Now I knew that she was in there, I wasn't going to give up.

I kept peering through the letterbox and shouting her name and telling her to answer the door. Then I saw a shadow at the top of the stairs. As the shadow descended I saw bare feet, then bare legs, then an over-sized t-shirt and then her face. Her movements were like an old woman's. I was so glad that she couldn't see my expression when I first caught sight of her because I gasped in shock. But for the fact that I knew it was her, I probably would not have believed it. Her hair, which she was so proud of, was a complete mess. It looked like it hadn't been washed or brushed in weeks. She looked absolutely gaunt and the t-shirt was stuck to her skeletal frame. This is probably what shocked me most; she was just so thin.

I had intended giving out to her for not getting in touch with me, but as soon as I saw her I knew that something was badly wrong. She let me in and turned to go straight back to her bedroom without saying a word. I followed her in silence. She got back into bed and looked straight at me. I had to prise every single word out of her and eventually she told me that she had no energy and couldn't face getting up anymore. I found out that she had been in that state for almost two months and I felt so guilty. There was me, annoyed with her for not getting in touch, and all the time she was lying in bed going through agony. She had managed to hide it from her family by saying she was travelling a lot with work and pre-programming her computer to send automatic emails to them every few days.

I knew that she was sick and I knew she needed more help than I would be able to give. I persuaded her to let me ring her GP and ask him to make a home visit. I promised that I would stay with her. While we were waiting I went to make a cup of coffee and discovered that there was no coffee, no milk, no sugar. In fact, there was no fresh food and *very little tinned or dried food. I wondered how long it had been since she had had a cooked meal or anything nourishing to eat. I tidied up the place and made a list of things to get in the shop. I wanted her doctor to see her as I did – dishevelled, unkempt, distracted, apathetic and malnourished. She spoke very slowly and nothing she said was terribly optimistic. It was as if she had resigned herself to this existence without any hope of a future. It was hard to believe that the girl lying in front of me was my friend, who was vivacious, funny, smart, beautiful, sociable and dependable.*

I felt so damn bad that I hadn't done more or tried harder instead of giving up on her. The doctor diagnosed severe depression within a matter of minutes and prescribed anti-depressants for her. He also made an appointment for her to see a psychiatrist. Over the next few weeks I called almost every day, brought her meals, went with her to her appointments, did shopping and gave the house a clean. I didn't make a big deal of it and I felt good to be helping. As the months went by I could see parts of my friend begin to emerge. She wasn't staying in bed anymore; she came out with me on walks; she started paying attention to her appearance and began going out again. I spoke to some of our other friends and between us we rallied around to make sure that she knew she wasn't on her own and that we were all proud of how she doing.

The final milestone came seven months later when she went back to work. It was a great day not only for her, but also for her family and friends, who had supported her. A gang of us went out for a meal that night to celebrate and it was just like old times. I looked at her that night when she wasn't watching and I could feel a tear run down my face. She had battled and she had won. She had come full circle.

―◄O►―

It helps to read up on depression so that you can educate yourself about things you should and should not do, issues you may need to be aware of, and also what you can do to help. Ignorance induces fear, but knowledge provides understanding. The best thing you can give your friend is emotional support. It's not uncommon for people to lie about being depressed. If you suspect a friend may be depressed, don't take what they say at face value, even though it may be easier for you to.

If your friend tells you he or she is fine when you suspect they are not, say so. Try to get them to talk about how they are feeling and don't be afraid to suggest they seek professional help. Reassure them that you don't think any differently of them because of this and if you have suffered from depression yourself at any time, share your experience with them. You will be a beacon of hope in this dark time for them; proof that people come through the illness. Whatever you do, don't ignore the

231

symptoms. Your intervention has the potential to really make a difference.

Every depressed person needs to talk to someone who will listen, without passing judgement or giving an opinion. This is probably one of the reasons psychotherapy proves to be an effective way to treat depression. Although your intention may be good, never try to talk a depressed person out of how they are feeling, or trivialise their thinking. Often their feelings may be irrational and pessimistic, but telling them they are wrong will serve only to silence them and possibly the only source they use to unload.

Always be on the lookout for talk of suicide; this is something that *always* has to be taken seriously. Someone who is depressed doesn't say or do things for attention. If your friend is talking about "ending it all" or saying they wish they were dead, tell someone, preferably a healthcare professional. You are not betraying your friend's confidence by doing this; you could be literally saving their life. Pay particular attention to any sudden change in mood, perking up or peacefulness in the person – these can signal a burst of energy that will enable them to follow up on suicide plans *(you can read more about this in Chapter 9)*. Additionally, enlist the help and support of your friend's family and other friends. Perhaps even suggest meeting with some of them to devise ways of helping your friend. It's possible the depression is being concealed from family, particularly if your friend is single and living alone.

Your friend's depression is not your fault and it is highly unlikely that anything you do will be sufficient to make them better. However, by offering support and understanding you help to make it less of a "shame" to get treatment. Depression can be a chameleon of an illness; each person has different triggers, different causes, different symptoms and different reactions. There is nothing wrong with asking direct questions if you do not understand something your friend says or does. Depression is an illness and cannot be cured overnight. However, it can be cured and your friend will return to the person he or she was before getting sick. They will have clarity once again and they will remember those who stuck around when it would have been easier not to.

How to Recognise Depression in a Friend

- Your calls, texts and/or emails may go unanswered
- They will withdraw socially
- They may stop partaking in activities such as going to the gym
- They may start talking pessimistically about things
- They will likely say there is nothing wrong when there clearly is
- They will start to let domestic chores slip
- They may take less of an interest in their personal appearance
- Their normal behaviour may change
- They may be more irritable and stressed
- Their perception of things may become irrational

Things You Can Do to Help

- Be sympathetic and understanding

- Try and convince them to get help

- Read up on depression

- Don't judge

- Give reassurance and encouragement

- Don't try to cheer them up

- Don't try to force your friend to do what you think she or he needs to do

- Don't get angry with them

- Don't tell them that things are not as bad as they seem

- Don't try to bribe them to make an effort

- Don't be patronising or condescending

- Constantly reinforce the fact that depression is treatable

- Don't be critical of how they are behaving

- Help out with chores – cooking, cleaning, shopping, etc.

- Be there for them during treatment and recovery

9

Suicide

"If mental health becomes more of an everyday issue that matters to us all, then the stigma attached to getting help can be reduced. While Irish society will continue to experience considerable change and face new challenges ahead, a mentally healthier Irish society will be much better able to cope."

NATIONAL OFFICE FOR SUICIDE PREVENTION

Depression is often associated with suicide, and for good reason. Worldwide there is one suicide every minute and one suicide attempt every three minutes. According to data from the National Office for Suicide Prevention in Ireland, more people in the world die from suicide than from armed conflict.

It is never easy to believe, or indeed accept, that a person you love would ever consider committing suicide. However, depression is known to cloud judgement, distort thinking and cause irrational perceptions. It is not uncommon for a previously rational and logical person to see suicide as the only escape from the agony and turmoil they are feeling as a result of depression. Mostly they do not think about the consequences of their actions and concerns about work, family or friends have no meaning.

For them, suicide is the obvious choice; the only positive step they can think of.

People who have suicidal thoughts, and indeed those who actually go on to commit suicide, are, for the most part, ordinary people faced with what they perceive as extraordinary problems, who cannot stand life and decide it is not worth living anymore. They can see no other way to stop the despair or to regain control. However, it is not uncommon for them to be ambivalent about their decision, which provides a window of opportunity in which other people can help. There are some common warning signs of suicide which, when acted upon, can very often save lives.

Common Signs

- Talks about ending it all
- Statements questioning the point of living
- Preoccupation with death and dying
- Self-harming
- Preparing for death; e.g. gets things in order such as making a will, writing letters to family and friends or sorting financial affairs
- Has had recent severe losses
- Has attempted suicide before
- Indulges in unnecessary risk-taking behaviour or hobbies

- Loses interest in hobbies, work, school, etc.
- Suddenly visits or calls people they care about
- Gives things away
- Has trouble eating or sleeping
- Withdraws from friends and/or social activities
- Loses interest in their personal appearance
- Increases their use of alcohol or drugs

What To Do

- Be alert: you should be especially aware of sudden mood changes where the person appears happier, calmer or peaceful. The risk of suicide is often greatest when a depressed person appears to be getting better. However, this may mean that they finally have the energy to take suicidal action. They often appear relieved and at peace – this is because they have finally taken the decision and have enough energy to act upon it.

- Take action: look to remove things that could enable the person to commit suicide such as knives and, if applicable, guns, from the reach of the person. Always be on the lookout for stockpiles of pills of any type.

- Do not be sworn to secrecy or confidentiality: you cannot assume this responsibility on your own and you will need support from other people such as heath professionals, family members and friends.

- Do not under-react: a person does not threaten suicide as a way of getting attention; they see it as a way of stopping the pain.

- Take the person seriously, stay calm and listen. Accept how the person is feeling, be non-judgemental and do not patronise or lecture.

- Do not look or act shocked: this will cause the person to clam up.

- Offer reassurance: explain that stress suicide is a permanent solution to a temporary problem. Emphasise that help is available and things will get better, but do not be condescending.

- Be direct: talk openly and matter-of-factly about suicide; try to find out if the person has a specific plan. Voice your personal concerns to the person and list the reasons that make you believe he or she is close to suicide.

- Get involved: be available for the person, show that you are interested in how they feel.

- Be attentive: make eye contact and sit close to the person.

Feelings

As a non-depressed and non-suicidal person, it can be difficult to understand the thoughts and feelings of someone who is. Sometimes it can be hard to understand and empathise when you don't know what you are dealing with. These are some common feelings:

- They feel utter despair and are unable to see a way out

- They cannot stop the pain and turmoil they are in

- Their thoughts are jumbled and they are unable to think clearly

- They cannot rise above how they are feeling

- They feel they have no control

- They wonder if they are losing their mind

- They can see no future

- They are unable to make decisions

- They are often angry with themselves for feeling as they do

- They see themselves as worthless and feel hopeless

- They cannot function normally or work

- They cannot make the sadness go away

Myths about Suicide

Myth: *People who talk about suicide never go through with it.*

Fact: It is estimated that eight out of ten people who commit suicide spoke about their intent before killing themselves.

Myth: *Suicide often happens without the person giving any warning.*

Fact: Almost everyone who commits suicide has given some clue or warning.

Myth: *Suicide is just a way to get attention.*

Fact: Those who are planning to commit suicide are not doing it to get attention; they are doing it to stop their pain.

Myth: *There is nothing you can do to stop someone who decides to commit suicide.*

Fact: Most people are very ambivalent about suicide; most people who commit suicide don't want to die, they just want their pain to stop.

Myth: *Only crazy people commit suicide.*

Fact: More often than not, ordinary people commit suicide over ordinary problems.

Myth: *People who attempt suicide and fail will not try again.*

Fact: Previous attempts are one of the known risk factors of suicide.

Myth: *Only weak people commit suicide.*

Fact: Many "strong" people die by suicide.

Myth: *Only adults think about suicide.*

Fact: In Ireland suicide is the leading cause of death for young people aged fifteen to twenty-four.

Myth: *A suicidal person does not want help.*

Fact: Many people who are suicidal reach out for help.

Myth: *Talking about suicide to a suicidal person will put the idea into their head and make them more determined to do it.*

Fact: It is important to talk about suicide with people who are suicidal.

Myth: *When people who are suicidal feel better, they are no longer suicidal.*

Fact: Sometimes suicidal people feel better because they have decided to die by suicide, and may feel a sense of relief that the pain will soon be over.

Myth: *Drugs and alcohol play no part in suicide.*

Fact: Very often, people who commit suicide are under the influence of drugs and/or alcohol.

241

10

Professionally Speaking

"We are made wise not by the recollection of our
past, but by the responsibility for our future."

GEORGE BERNARD SHAW

During and after my illness I had many questions I
wanted answered. Some were to do with the illness;
others were to do with the issues surrounding it. In my
quest to understand my illness, I took on the approach of
a researcher. I dissected study after study, textbook after
textbook and website after website. However, although I
had researched it thoroughly and read about it
voraciously, I still wanted to know more. I wanted to
know what those who dealt with depression on a daily
basis thought. In this chapter, three professionals, who
are each involved with depression on a daily basis in
different ways through their work, answer some of the
most common questions about depression. They address
the signs, the symptoms, the problems, the treatments,
and also give practical advice. They also address the issue
of stigma, the lack of public awareness, the need for

Karina Colgan

greater education and what, in their opinion, is the most progressive way forward.

Dr James Lee is founder and director of medical group Primacare. As a GP, he is often the first point of contact for a depressed person. He is familiar with all the signs, symptoms, types and treatments for depression, and offers a medical perspective and practical advice.

Sandra Hogan is Public Relations Officer for Aware, a voluntary organisation that was set up in 1985 to assist those who are affected by depression. Aware depends on fund-raising for 80 per cent of its operating costs, which include manning a national helpline, running support groups and educational programmes for schools. She is familiar with all aspects of depression.

John Lonergan is Governor of Mountjoy Prison, Dublin. Not surprisingly, with one in four prisoners having been in-patients with mental illness, approximately 40 per cent having contact with psychiatric services and a very high percentage openly displaying symptoms of depression, he not only sees the effects of depression on a daily basis, but he also deals with the sad issue of suicide.

Dr James Lee,
Founder and Director, Primacare Group

In your opinion does stigma still surround the issue of depression?

Yes, it does. Many people suffer from depression but rarely speak openly about it for fear of being stigmatised.

Why do you think depression exists in a progressive country like Ireland?

Depression is not fully understood and ignorance induces fear.

What, in your opinion, can be done to eradicate stigma?

I think that prominent people in society coming forward and speaking openly about their depression would help enormously. Depression also needs to become "fashionable" if stigma is to be reduced.

What are the most common signs of depression people present with?

While some people present with depression, there is a range of other presentations from anxiety, insomnia, alcohol and drug abuse to physical symptoms.

What do you think are the biggest problems facing people with depression?

In my opinion, acceptance of the condition is the biggest problem facing depressed people. Another big problem people face is the lack of support services.

Is there a distinction made between men and women in relation to depression?

Within society I think it is quite possibly the case. However, within the medical profession there is no distinction made; it is an illness that affects both sexes. In my experience, women are more likely to admit to depression while men are more likely to commit suicide.

What do you think are the biggest problems facing those affected by depression in a family member?

There are a number of problems those affected by a loved one being depressed face. However, I think one of the biggest relates to getting the depressed person to seek and accept help. Family members also face a lack of support services for people in their position.

Do you think there are enough support mechanisms in place for depressed people?

Most definitely not – particularly in the area of counselling services such as Cognitive Behavioural Therapy.

Do you think there is a difference in care between the public and private health care systems?

Unfortunately, yes. Private care is much better but extremely expensive, which puts it beyond the reach of many. There is a large role for the voluntary sector as there is not enough government funding for mental health problems.

What, in your opinion, causes depression?

I believe a mixture of nature and nurture. There is a genetic tendency, which can be triggered by a wide range of adverse environmental factors such as births, deaths, trauma, financial and relationship problems, etc. In my opinion nature is a more important factor than nurture. If some people are predisposed to depression, it is important they understand the condition and what measures to take to deal with it as soon as it begins to recur.

Statistics show that 80 per cent of suicides are attributed to depression. Why do you think this is?

It stands to reason that if a person is feeling low then they are more likely to take their own lives. However, I believe that an understanding of the condition, acceptance of it and effective treatments could lower the suicide figures.

Do you think employers recognise depression as they would any illness?

I find that many patients do not want to put a psychological diagnosis on a cert, so it certainly appears many employers do not view it as they would any other illness. Patients are afraid that a diagnosis of depression will jeopardise future promotion and employment prospects.

Statistics show that 400,000 people suffer from depression every year in Ireland. Do you think the general public are as informed about depression as they could or should be?

I think that the general public are not as informed as they should be, which is a pity. Greater awareness would certainly lead to earlier intervention and more effective treatment, which in turn would lower this statistic.

Do you think there is enough advertising surrounding depression?

I am not sure that advertising in the conventional sense would be a good idea, but greater exposure and discussion in the media in general would be most helpful. This would make depression more acceptable and understood by the general population.

Do you there is a general lack of education about depression?

Yes, most definitely. I believe it would be useful if the issue of depression could be taught as a part of the Social, Personal and Health Education (SPHE) curriculum in schools. I also think that celebrities could play a role, particularly for younger people. Additionally, it is important that patients who suffer from depression are educated about the condition, so that they can take measures to deal with it and avoid it in the future.

Do you think that government could do more?

Yes, particularly in the economic sense. However, it is also important for society in general to engage with the problem. I believe that leaders and celebrities have as big a role to play as politicians.

If you had funds to channel into depression, what area of the illness would you concentrate on?

In general I would put money into support services such as psychological treatments. There is also a lot of research to be done, particularly in the areas of genetics and pharmacological treatments.

What advice would you give to someone who thinks they may be depressed?

Talk to someone you trust and seek professional help. Keeping it to yourself only makes it worse.

What advice would you give to someone who is depressed and is reluctant to seek help?

You are not alone; a lot of people have this condition. There are effective treatments that your GP can explain and prescribe for you, as well as being able to talk to him or her in confidence.

What advice would you give to someone who is afraid to discuss this issue with his or her employer?

Employers may not the best people to discuss this condition with. I think initially it should only be discussed with someone you trust. Don't talk to your employer if you feel they may not be sympathetic. On the other hand, if your employer is sympathetic, he or she can be an extremely useful source of support.

What advice would you give employers in relation to dealing with an employee who is depressed?

The best advice is to be supportive. It is generally the case that those who are supportive find that they will have a grateful and productive worker for life.

What advice would you give to the parent of a depressed teenager?

Seek help. This is often difficult, as teenagers like to be independent. It can be very useful to enlist the help of someone in the field of the same age. It is important not to be judgemental with teenagers and to concentrate on gaining their confidence. Threats of suicide or suicidal comments should always be taken seriously and professional help immediately sought.

Loneliness, despair, apathy, shame, embarrassment, hopelessness are all feelings commonly felt by a person who is depressed. What, by way of encouragement, would you say to someone feeling like this?

All of these are negative emotions that with treatment can be turned into positives. I think that informing the patient that all of the above feelings are common in depressed patients and can be abolished with treatment, will offer encouragement. So too will the fact that they are not alone.

What symptoms, in particular, should people pay attention to?

Constant low mood is not a normal state; it can be changed with the right treatment. Feeling that life is not enjoyable any more, or a constant feeling of dread, are also good indicators of depression. Suicidal tendencies should always, without exception, be treated seriously.

What are the most common types of depression you deal with?

I deal with both endogenous (originating from within the body) and reactive (as a result of external factors and life events). As I work with young families, one of the most common types of depression I see is post-natal depression.

In your experience, how long does depression usually last?

It has no definite timeframe. For many people it will last for a few months, although it can last longer. With treatment it can be improved within as little time as a month.

In an ideal world, what should depression mean?

I think that depression should be looked at as a positive. People who suffer from depression have attributes such as empathy and generosity that others lack. Additionally, their insights enable them to excel in the humanities such as music and literature, as well as in sciences and mathematics. The list of great leaders who have suffered from depression is endless *(see Chapter 13).*

One in three people will suffer from depression at some point in their lives, either directly or indirectly. What do you think can be done to reduce this?

We cannot eliminate depression completely, nor would we want to, for the reason that some sadness is part of the human condition. It is only when it becomes a burden that the patient cannot cope with, that we need to intervene. Sometimes, I think that all thinking people must become depressed from time to time. The challenge is to learn from the experience and turn it into a positive.

Sandra Hogan,
Public Relations Officer, Aware

What are the biggest problems facing people with depression?

Stigma is one of the biggest issues. Where someone knows that something is amiss, they can still be reluctant to seek help for fear of being judged or labelled. Additionally, where someone is in treatment for depression, they may be reluctant to tell family and friends for fear of their reaction. This effectively cuts off a vital means of support for anyone who is going through or endeavouring to recover from a depression. Alongside stigma, access to the most appropriate treatment is also a huge issue.

Why does stigma still surround the issue of depression?

Unfortunately stigma still has a huge role to play in how depression is viewed. It is extremely unfortunate that this is the case: stigma and the fear of being labelled or judged by peers can, and does, prevent many people from coming forward for help and support.

Why does stigma exist in a progressive country like Ireland?

There are many reasons why stigma still persists in Ireland. Attitudes to mental ill health have always differed from attitudes to physical health. This may have to do with the fact that physical health problems are viewed as being "of the body", whereas mental health issues are "of the mind" and are perhaps understood as affecting the very core of the person. Given that mental health is less readily understood than physical health, it leaves space for a vacuum to exist where misunderstanding and myth can thrive. There are many health awareness campaigns for common physical problems yet, until 2007, there was no national awareness campaign for mental health.

In past times, many individuals with mental health problems were cared for in asylums. The very word "asylum" means "safe place", yet because most of these places were built on the outskirts of towns and many individuals who were admitted to asylums were under long-term care, it meant that people with mental health difficulties were effectively removed from society. That in itself created an inequality. Of course, the irony is that anyone in Ireland can experience a metal health problem, so it is appalling that this stigma still persists.

What, in your opinion, can be done to eradicate stigma?

A national mental health awareness campaign, which underlines the fact that mental health problems are common, can affect anyone, and can usually be recovered from, is absolutely necessary. This campaign should also focus on targeting stigma and the way in which even our everyday language and behaviour can contribute to stigma. It is important too, that awareness of mental health is incorporated into the national curriculum at primary school level so that from a young age, people grow up knowing that it is wrong to judge someone who experiences depression or other mental ill-health.

What are the most common signs of depression you see?

The most common signs of depression include disturbed sleep; changes in appetite; low energy; withdrawal from life and loss of interest in hobbies, work, family, etc. Thoughts of death or suicide may also be common. Many people don't realise that depression can have physical symptoms such as aches and pains associated with stress or anxiety (e.g. tummy pains, headaches, chest pains).

What, in your opinion, causes depression?

There are many factors that can result in depression. For some individuals depression will result from a traumatic life event, e.g. bereavement, relationship breakdown, financial difficulties or job loss. It is really important in this instance that we do not judge other people based on how we think we would feel if such a thing happened to us. For example, the loss of a job may be a minor concern for one individual but may present a major upset for someone else. Others may be born with a tendency to depression, which may be triggered only at a later stage in life.

Many of the symptoms of depression can be common during the ups and downs of everyday life: the difference between the usual "ups and downs" and depression itself is that the latter is *enduring* in its nature, so that there will be little or no respite from symptoms. Another important thing to acknowledge is that one does not have to *feel* depressed in order to *be* depressed: that feeling is just one of the eight main symptoms associated with the condition and may not be present for everyone.

Is there a distinction made between males and females with depression?

Females are generally more likely to acknowledge (to themselves or to others) that something is wrong, whereas men generally try to hide depression. This is very much linked in with the idea that "men don't cry" and that men are "strong". We really need to examine and change our attitudes to this and to look at the way in which we all, deliberately or otherwise, perpetuate this idea. Although experts estimate that women are three to four times more likely to experience depression, men are more likely to die by suicide. Women tend to have more protective factors in their life such as close, confiding relationships with other women, whereas this is not always the case for men. Subsequently, this means that men may be more likely to struggle on with depression alone.

Karina Colgan

What are the biggest problems facing those affected by depression in a family member?

It can be extremely difficult to support a loved one through depression, but it can also be a hugely rewarding experience and one that deepens and cements the relationship. It is estimated that for every one person who experiences depression, up to five other family members/friends will be impacted on. Many family members will be impacted to such an extent that they need help and support themselves. Aware recognises the key role family and friends play and offers support to these individuals too, via its loCall Helpline and also support groups specifically for family members.

Do you think there are enough support mechanisms in place for depressed people?

Absolutely not. Most of the supports that are in place are run by voluntary organisations like Aware and The Samaritans. There has to be an onus on the state to provide adequate mental health services in this country, so that anyone who has a mental health difficulty has somewhere to turn and, equally important, knows exactly where to turn.

Do you think there is a difference in care between the public and private healthcare systems?

Yes, there is a difference across the board and this is true in relation to mental health as well.

Statistics show that 80 per cent of suicides are attributed to depression. Why do you think this is?

This is mostly due to the fact that many people do not come forward for help and support and, even where they do, they may not always have access to the most appropriate form of treatment for them. Suicidal thoughts, feelings and behaviour can be a part of depression for many people, but the majority can come through these feelings with the right support. Alcohol also has a significant role to play in many suicides and some individuals with depression may turn to alcohol in a bid to ease their symptoms. Alcohol is itself a depressant, so aggravates any underlying mood disorder. It is also a dis-inhibitor so it can lower the individual's inhibitions towards self-anger, self-aggression and self-harm.

Do you think employers recognise depression as they would any illness?

Most employers are not sure how to deal with depression in the workplace. Some of the bigger companies have employee counselling and assistance programmes, but I'm not sure how efficient these are, i.e. whether staff use them or what the follow-up care is like. There is no standard for how employers handle depression in the workplace.

Do you think the general public are as informed about depression as they could or should be?

No. There is little awareness of the signs and symptoms of depression, how common it is, or where to turn to for help.

Do you think there is enough advertising surrounding depression?

No. Aware holds Depression Awareness Week Nationwide (DAWN) each January, but this is usually limited to a moderate radio and press campaign due to resources. One-off ads are also included in various publications during the year, but much more is needed.

Do you there is a general lack of education about depression?

Yes. Aware runs a secondary schools awareness programme called "Beat the Blues", as well as an educational programme for interested parties called "Beyond the Blues" and regular public lectures. However, there really needs to be general and large-scale education about depression.

What more do you think could be done by government?

More funding on all levels: awareness, education, services, as well as a general commitment to making mental health a central political issue.

If you had funds to channel into depression, what area of the illness would you concentrate on?

Awareness is key to improving knowledge of depression among the general public: this will also impact on the stigma as well as the numbers coming forward for help and support. Additionally, increased funding for existing support services is essential.

What advice would you give to someone who thinks they may be depressed?

Contact Aware on loCall 1890 303 302 for information and support and get a correct diagnosis from your GP. The latter is essential – once you know what you are dealing with, management of the condition is easier, and recovery is possible.

What advice would you give to someone who is depressed and is reluctant to seek help?

It depends on the reason for the reluctance. Is it fear of being stigmatised? If so, access information online at www.aware.ie or contact the confidential Aware loCall Helpline. It can definitely help to speak with someone who has a real appreciation of how difficult dealing with depression is, so making a call to the Helpline can be a really good start point. As with other Aware services, the Helpline is strictly confidential.

What advice would you give to someone who is afraid to discuss this issue with his or her employer?

Whether or not a person tells their employer is their own decision. It is a good idea to discuss the issue with someone close whom you can trust first of all and weigh up the pros and cons of telling your employer. If you do decide to go ahead, then it is wise to tell your boss that you wish to find ways to deal with your condition that will have least impact on your job. It is possible to look at job-sharing, taking a period of leave while a temp looks after your duties and looking at how to address particular stressors, which may aggravate your condition. A knowledge of support services and commitment to utilising them when needed is also a good way to show employers that you are dealing with your condition as responsibly as you can.

What advice would you give employers in relation to dealing with an employee who is depressed?

Learn about the condition so that you know what you and your employee are dealing with. Work with your employee to find ways to enable them to continue their work while dealing with their condition at the same time if this is possible. Aware publishes a leaflet entitled "Depression in the Workplace" and this looks at various ways in which colleagues can support someone with depression. It really is in the best interests of everyone involved to deal with the depression responsibly.

Loneliness, despair, apathy, shame, embarrassment, hopelessness are all feelings commonly felt by a person who is depressed. What by way of encouragement would you say to someone feeling like this?

Although you may feel that you are the only person in the world who has ever felt this way, this is not true. Depression is a disabling condition and can take away all hope for the future, but it is possible to recover from it with the right help and support. There is no reason for you to be ashamed or embarrassed: this is something that can happen to any one of us at any time in our life and it is in no way your fault. If you had a physical illness you would seek help and advice from your doctor and it should be no different with depression. Help and support is available for you: do not suffer in silence because you are not alone and you can recover.

What symptoms should people pay attention to?

Any of the symptoms of depression that last for a period of weeks with little or no respite should be noted. These include: disturbed sleep or appetite; low energy; withdrawal from family/friends; feelings of sadness, anxiety or boredom; negativity about the future; low self-esteem; loss of interest in hobbies; physical aches and pains which cannot be explained and, of course, thoughts of death or suicide.

Do depressed people tend to turn to alcohol, prescribed medication and/or illicit substances in an effort to block out the depression?

Not everyone who experiences depression will use alcohol or other substances, but it is important to remember that these things may be used if someone is not getting the help and support they need to manage the depression. Sometimes we might think that alcohol aids relaxation and relieves symptoms of anxiety after a difficult day. Unfortunately alcohol is actually a depressant and so can aggravate any underlying tendency towards depression. In cases of binge drinking (four drinks or more in one session) the depressive and dis-inhibiting effect of alcohol is increased. It can reduce inhibitions to self-anger, self-aggression and self-harm. The use of illicit drugs is also important as many of these have a very negative impact on mental health especially in people under twenty-five. (The brain reaches full development around the age of twenty-five and early research suggests that the impact of illicit drugs on the brain and mental health may be more acute in younger people.) Symptoms such as paranoia, hallucinations and psychosis can result from even those drugs which are viewed as being more "mainstream" or socially acceptable e.g. cannabis, cocaine.

John Lonergan,
Governor, Mountjoy Prison

In your opinion, what percentage of the prison population suffers from depression?

There is a very high prevalence of depression here. Given the stressful nature of the environment, this is not surprising. One in four people here have been in-patients with mental illness, and approximately 40 per cent have had contact with psychiatric services. A high percentage of people openly express feelings of depression.

What are the most common signs of depression you see?

Little or no motivation, negative feelings, staying in bed, apathy, going sick, are the most common signs. There can be a general air of hopelessness, which is often caused by separation from family and loved ones. Equally, there is often a feeling of loneliness. Not only do people often feel isolated by the illness, but the fact that they may be locked up for fifteen or sixteen hours every day also contributes to this. A small percentage of people self-harm.

What treatments are available to depressed people?

A pre-condition of help is that the person must recognise they have a problem and seek help. A lot of people don't look for help and instead try to cope with it alone. We have good support infrastructure through medical, psychological and chaplaincy services. Depression is a huge problem and we have doctors who treat the problem medically and clinically. We have a good in-house psychiatric service and also a twenty-four-hour nurse service. In addition to a direct line to The Samaritans, there is a "listening scheme" in operation where prisoners can talk to other prisoners about their problems and about how they are feeling.

What, in your opinion, causes depression?

Many factors and also sometimes it is a medical reason. Depression is often a reaction to life; personal circumstances and addiction are all contributory factors.

I also believe a lack of self-esteem is a factor. For some people, life is a constant struggle. Circumstances can change and so too can depression. I believe it is very much about the inward feelings of the person we see on the outside. It is very important that people do not make the mistake of assuming someone is fine from their outward views.

Nature versus nurture – what are your views?

I think both are crucial and have major influences on our lives. Nature cannot be ignored; I see illness pass from generation-to-generation here. However, I believe that nurture plays a far more significant role. What happens us is more likely to leave marks than nature. We have control over nurture; we can learn how to react. The area of rejection is a huge cause of depression. So many areas can, and do, change. We cannot eliminate nature, but should err on the side of nurturing. The absence of real human love can have devastating effects. For example, in prisons the most dramatic punishment is that of solitary confinement. Many people feel isolated in today's world. As human beings we have an innate need to connect and belong.

Do you think some people are predisposed to depression?

Although there can be no question that nature sometimes plays a part, I believe we create the environment that creates depression.

Have you seen people appear to recover and relapse?

Sometimes, like addiction, people relapse as part of the journey to recovery. People must recognise and accept the illness. They must also accept their reality and until they do these things they cannot get on the road to recovery. We often find a person who is doing well experiencing a personal setback and going straight back to square one. For me, relapse is part of the human journey in coping with the journey of life itself.

Statistics show that 80 per cent of suicides are attributed to depression. As someone who deals with deaths from suicide, do you think those who died were obviously depressed or did they hide it?

In my experience of suicide over the years, both in and out of prison, I would say it is somewhere in the region of fifty-fifty. There is no doubt that depression is a major contributory factor and many people who commit suicide certainly have issues around depression. Conversely, I have also been aware of people who have committed suicide and not shown any outward signs of being depressed. I think sometimes we focus a little too much on preventing suicide at the expense of missing the bigger picture. Staff/people need to pick up on this. This is part of our staff induction training and we are also undertaking research at the moment with the HSE in relation to staff needs, help and intervention regarding suicide. Our connection with The Samaritans has made a significant contribution to reducing the number of suicides in prison.

Do you think employers recognise depression as they would any other illness?

No, I don't think they do. They suffer from the same prejudices as anyone else. Depression is not perceived as something "normal". There is a taboo and a sense of being uncomfortable with it. Illnesses such as the 'flu are readily accepted as being an illness. If an employee has a broken arm, it is easy to ask how their arm is. However, if an employee is known to be suffering from depression, employers tend not to ask how their depression is.

As an employer, how do you deal with staff who suffer from depression?

In modern Ireland, depression with staff today is a completely new issue. In the old days, for example, the medical service took care of all staff medical needs. These days, staff look after their own healthcare. We have prison officers who are trained in the area of staff support. As depression generally stems from issues around personal circumstances, it is my opinion that staff are not likely to disclose they are suffering from depression. I think the main monitor of depression is attendance, or rather lack of it. Other than this it is difficult to gauge any kind of percentage figure as not everyone admits to being depressed.

Do you think the general public is as informed about depression as it could or should be?

Goodness no, absolutely not. There is certain ignorance around the issues, reality and consequences of depression. A cynicism exists, whereby people who are depressed are not expected to miss work. It is not perceived as a "real" illness and can be very difficult to cope with. As a society there is no question we lack knowledge. Depression can affect anyone and can be an absolute scourge to those affected.

Do you think there is enough advertising surrounding depression?

The support groups that exist are great and "normalise" depression. However, there is still a huge amount of work to be done. There should be a drive on preventative measures aimed at families, communities and hospitals. Early prevention could well eliminate or certainly greatly reduce the need for hospital care. Depression is an area that requires and demands far more awareness about symptoms and solutions.

Do you think stigma still exists around this illness?

Without question stigma is a major factor when it comes to depression. I believe we will never get a proper response to the illness until we tackle and eliminate stigma. People still perceive depression as a failure. The very word "depression" is often used flippantly, but not too often seriously.

What more do you think could and should be done by government?

Depression is very much a human issue. It should not be compartmentalised. There should be the same level of education about depression that there is around other illnesses. Depression today is like TB was in times past, spoken about in hushed tones out of embarrassment. Although we are more enlightened now, I believe we still have a long way to go. We need to tackle the core problem and this can only be addressed through greater education.

Depression is normal and can be overcome. Resources should be put into creating a greater awareness. It would be money well spent and would also lessen the need for long-term hospitalisation. As well as the impact depression has on a person's quality of life, it must be remembered that it also has huge consequences for the family, for work and for the community. Often it is those closest to depressed people who suffer most. The consequences of depression can be as profound as the consequences of alcohol or drug addiction. We tend to forget family members.

If you had funds to channel into depression, what area of the illness would you concentrate on?

I would focus on awareness in an effort to de-stigmatise the illness. Regardless of who or what you are, depression is a reality and people need to be made aware of this. Some kind of infrastructure needs to be put in place to help people deal with and overcome depression. However, there is no doubt that this will continue to be an uphill battle until stigma is eradicated.

In an ideal world, what would depression mean?

It would be a normal illness and recognised as a reality of life and its journey. The reality of being human is that we are not perfect. Depression would be just a normal issue we deal with and is dealt with on the basis of normality.

11

Stigma and Myths
about Depression

**"Mental illness is nothing to be ashamed
of, but stigma and bias shames us all."**

BILL CLINTON

Stigma

Stigma n – *the shame or disgrace attached to something
regarded as socially unacceptable.*

Paedophiles are stigmatised; rapists are stigmatised; drug
pushers are stigmatised; and rightly so. What these people
do is socially unacceptable and they should be ashamed and
socially disgraced. However, quite incredibly, society also
chooses to place those who suffer from depression and
mental illness into this category. Without exception,
everyone I spoke with when writing this book cited stigma as
being one of the biggest problems facing people who are
depressed. How such a common illness is perceived as such
a social threat beggars belief.

This dangerous misconception prevents people who are
depressed from seeking help for fear of being judged or

labelled. It incites feelings of shame and embarrassment and contributes to the burden of a depressed person who, in addition to having to cope with the illness, also feels the need to keep it a secret from family and friends. Stigma fuels negative and incorrect assumptions about depression, stemming primarily from a lack of education and awareness about the illness.

I also include some key points from the National Office of Suicide Prevention's comprehensive 2007 study on the public's awareness and attitudes to mental health in Ireland. For me, its findings made disturbing reading.

Depressed people often have to contend with more than just their illness. The social stigma that surrounds depression means that often those who are depressed feel compelled to hide the debilitating physical and emotional symptoms of their illness. This is not only wrong, it is dangerous, because it prevents them from seeking the help they so desperately need.

The Health Service Executive National Office for Suicide Prevention survey, *Mental Health in Ireland: Awareness and Attitudes*, confirmed, among other things, the extent of the problem both in relation to stigma and the public's understanding of mental health problems. Having studied the survey myself, and also through speaking with Geoff Day, Director of NOSP, it is profoundly clear that there needs to be a fundamental change in how mental illness is perceived by individuals, by government and by society.

Geoff Day says that the findings of the survey clearly indicated that significant levels of stigma continue to exist around the areas of depression and mental health problems. He pointed out that even in a progressive country like Ireland, depression and mental health problems are issues that are still spoken about in hushed tones behind closed doors. "Mental health problems are very real, very common and it is of paramount importance that they are talked about. There is a *huge* need to educate the people of Ireland about mental health. The reality is that many of us can – and do – experience mental health problems."

As I explain elsewhere in this book, this survey confirms that some people perceive me – as a depressed person – to be a "dangerous" individual from whom people should be "protected". Additionally, I should not be permitted to hold down an important job. I wonder what psychiatrists, scientists, doctors, neurosurgeons, police, pilots and judges who suffer from depression think about this?

Geoff Day says education would go a long way in eradicating views as divergent as these "notions that we need to be protected from people with mental health problems and that people with mental health problems are in fact dangerous. Fear of the unknown could be influencing these fears and could also underlie the admission by one-third of adults that they would find it difficult to talk to someone with mental health problems."

The stigma that surrounds depression often adds to the feelings of failure that already plague a depressed person. It serves to endorse their thoughts and consequently makes them feel even more alone, unloved and inadequate. This in turn stops them from seeking help or telling anyone. Depression is not known as the "lonely disease" for no reason.

As Geoff Day explains: "The most striking survey result for me is that 85 per cent of the population recognise that anyone can suffer from a mental illness. This shows good public awareness of the problem. However, the fact that 62 per cent would not want their employers or relatives to know shows that the stigma of mental illness is still very strong."

There can be no doubt – and this is coming not only from professionals, but also from someone who has been there and experienced it first-hand – that there needs to be a radical change in the way society views depression. In a progressive country like Ireland, our attitudes and perceptions about depression and mental illness belong in the Dark Ages. Depression is a very common illness that can affect anybody. It is treatable and most people recover from it in months rather than years. The greatest thing that differentiates depression from other common illnesses is its symptoms.

Depression is a real illness with real symptoms. Just because somebody doesn't "look" sick or have any obvious symptoms doesn't mean that they are not sick. Equally, somebody doesn't have to feel depressed to be depressed. There is no stigma attached to other common illnesses such as asthma or diabetes, primarily because sufferers have obvious symptoms, which make it easy for people to see they are sick. An asthmatic will never be told to "get a grip" or to "snap out of it", yet depressed people frequently hear this.

Why? The answer is simple: ignorance. It is the perception that is wrong, not the person suffering from depression.

A depressed person is often made to feel guilty by people who, through a lack of education, public awareness and social stigma, do not understand what depression really is. Depression is nobody's fault. In fact, as most people who have suffered from depression will tell you, it is not something they would wish on their worst enemy.

Nobody chooses to be depressed; it just happens. More importantly, it can happen to anyone, just like any other illness. Equally, like many illnesses, it can be treated and the person gets better. To apportion blame is not only wrong, it is damaging.

We have a responsibility, both as individuals and as part of a progressive society, to make a concerted effort to avoid stereotyping and labelling people because we don't understand their illness. Depression is not a personal weakness or moral flaw. It is not something to be ashamed of, and misconceptions need to be eliminated if we are to make progress in understanding it and eradicating erroneous and dangerous myths. When I asked Geoff what more should be done by government in the area of mental health, he replied, "we have good strategies in *Vision for Change* and *Reach Out*. What they both require is sustained implementation and, where necessary, appropriate funding."

In December 2007, current affairs programme *Prime Time* was instructed to issue an apology after allowing panellists to use the term "basket case" on four occasions during a programme aired by RTÉ on 30 August 2007.

In handing down its findings, the Broadcasting Complaints Commission said: *"The context in which the term 'basket case' was used could be considered to stigmatise people with mental illness and therefore was likely to cause offence."* The complaint was upheld in part under Section 24(2)(d)(taste & decency; Code of Programme Standards).

Society needs to be educated about depression and mental illness. This can only be done with commitment by government of more funding for education on all levels and also by making mental health a central political issue. Figures show that 20 to 30 per cent of all health disability is related to mental health problems, yet the funds assigned to mental health services from the national health falls far short of a comparable percentage.

There has to be a greater awareness of the illness and education and sustained advertising are areas that must be looked at. Information has to be easily accessible so that people can learn about the illness and also so that those suffering from it know where to go for help. However, there is little point in improving services without also working to address the stigma that stops people from availing of treatment. Research has shown that while one-third of Ireland's workforce has had depression, workers are reluctant to disclose depression to their employers for fear of negative consequences.

According to Geoff Day, ambivalence is a sign of a desire to live as well as to die. "Whilst it is necessary to explore why people want to die, in so doing the desire to live can be the factor which moves people away from suicide. Talking to friends, relatives or a health professional is important."

I conducted one of my many surveys among college students. The average age was twenty and the surveys were conducted anonymously. Some of the questions I asked related to the issue of stigma. Although the interviewees were very different individuals, their answers in relation to stigma were frighteningly similar.

- Answers to the question: "Would you hide being depressed from people?" included: "*Yes, because people think of you as different*"; "*Yes, because I would be afraid to tell people*"; "*Yes, most people are probably more depressed because of what people think*"; "*Yes, because I would be ashamed and embarrassed*"; "*Yes, you are regarded as 'odd'. People wonder what you have to be depressed about. Revealing you have depression would lead to you being pushed further out of a social group, which you may have felt you didn't really belong to anymore because of being depressed.*"

- Answers to the question: "What is your understanding of depression?" included: "*An imbalance of the brain that can destroy people*"; "*Even small things can upset you. You feel like you haven't a friend in the world*"; "*People feeling sorry for themselves"; "It's a sickness; just like cancer"; "Someone who feels alone in the world"; "It's feeling low and not knowing why or how to get better."*

- All students agreed that far more information should be made available. Answers to the question: "Do you think there is enough information about depression?" included: *"No, there isn't enough information about depression; nobody has a real understanding of it"; "No. Although most colleges have a guidance counsellor and chaplain who are available for support, they are badly advertised and it's hard to make an appointment to see them. I think education for young people should be a priority due to the high suicide rates among them"; "No. I think if people were better educated they would be able to seek the appropriate help"; "No. I only know what I hear and usually that's not very important. People tend to laugh at depression or think it's a cop-out"; "No, not many people know its symptoms or really know very little about it"; "No. It's an issue that people need to be made aware of. I think too many people have lost loved ones to depression because they didn't know they were sick"; "No. A lot of people who have depression don't know what their options are."*

Dispelling myths and eradicating stigma is the only way we are ever going to reach a better and informed understanding of depression. People are afraid of depression mostly because they simply don't understand it. Fear of the unknown is a very great fear, and if we feel threatened or uncomfortable with something, our natural reaction is to isolate it and remove our association with it. With depression, we should, as individuals and as a society, be doing the complete opposite, for knowledge brings understanding.

Geoff Day says: "Completed suicide is a permanent option even though many of our mental health concerns can be passing in nature, albeit overpowering at the time. It is important that those in difficulty try and understand that there is help from a range of sources, voluntary organisations and statutory mental health services."

Common Myths

Myth: Depression is a personal weakness.

Fact: Depression is a medical illness. Additionally, in view of the huge stigma that surrounds mental illness, seeking help for depression is an act of courage, not a weakness.

Myth: You can will depression to go away.

Fact: Depression cannot be willed away any more than diabetes or heart disease can. Depression is caused by chemical changes in the body that cannot be simply willed away.

Myth: Once you have depression you will never get better.

Fact: People with depression respond well to treatment with more than 80 per cent of individuals making a good recovery.

Myth: People should be able to snap out of it.

Fact: Is it possible to "snap out" of heart disease?

Myth: Depression results from a personality weakness or character flaw.

Fact: Depression has nothing to do with being weak. It results from changes in brain function.

Myth: It's normal for old people to be depressed.

Fact: Depression is not a normal part of the ageing process and although seniors do generally experience more of the events that can trigger depression, it is still not normal for older adults to be depressed simply by virtue of being elderly. Depression in older people is often undiagnosed, making it important that their family members be able to spot the symptoms.

Myth: Depression doesn't affect children and adolescents.

Fact: Research has shown that children and adolescents can, and do, suffer from depression. In Ireland approximately one in ten of all thirteen-to nineteen-year-olds have a depressive disorder and it is generally accepted that children under the age of twelve can develop bipolar disorder.

The highest rates of deliberate self-harm are among females aged fifteen to nineteen years. Suicide is now the single biggest killer of young men aged fifteen to twenty-four years with depression cited as the main reason for suicide in 80 per cent of cases.

Myth: Depression is not a "real" illness.

Fact: Clinical depression is a medical condition that affects an individual's mood, thoughts and body. Depression is caused by genetic and biological factors.

Myth: Depression is the same as getting the "blues".

Fact: This is like saying a common cold is the same as pneumonia. Most people will get a dose of the blues at some time or other, but not everyone will get depression. Depression is far more debilitating than the blues and lasts far longer. A person does not commit suicide because of a dose of the "blues".

Myth: Depressed people just lie around feeling sorry for themselves.

Fact: Some of the most prominent people with the brightest minds in history suffered from depression, including Sir Isaac Newton, Abraham Lincoln, Charles Darwin, Ludwig von Beethoven and Michelangelo. These people were not renowned for sitting around feeling sorry for themselves.

Myth: *Depression is something that only affects women.*

Fact: While it is true that women are three to four times more likely than men to suffer from depression, men are far more likely to die by suicide. Male depression is frequently under-reported because of the perception that to get depressed is to show weakness and also because men prefer to play "brave soldiers".

Myth: *Depression is not that common.*

Fact: Depression is one of the leading causes of disability worldwide and, according to the World Health Organisation, affects over 122 million people. Between 5 and 10 per cent of people in a community at any given time are in need of help for depression, and as much as 8 to 20 per cent of people carry the risk of developing depression in their lifetime. In Ireland depression affects one in four people. These are just a sample of statistics, which prove depression is not only common; it is a silent epidemic.

> *Myth:* *Talking about depression only makes it worse.*
>
> Fact: Talking about it can bring some relief and perhaps, more importantly, alert someone else to the problem and the need for professional help.
>
> **To conclude,** *"We must not be hampered by yesterday's myths in concentrating on today's needs."* *(Harold Geneen)* *Health Safety Executive National Office for Suicide Prevention, Awareness and Attitudes to Mental Health in Ireland, 2007*

Some of the findings of this report included:

- Six in ten adults would not want others knowing if they had a mental health problem.

- Six in ten do not believe people with mental health problems should do important jobs.

- Thirty-six per cent believed people with mental health problems are dangerous.

- Thirty-nine per cent believed they needed to be protected from such people.

- Thirty-three per cent would find it difficult to talk to someone with such problems.

- One in five believed the outlook for recovery is poor.

- Suicide, depression and alcoholism are said to be the most important mental health/mental health-related problems that need to be tackled in Ireland.

- One in five people stated that they care for or are related to someone with a mental health problem.

- Irish people seriously underestimated the prevalence of mental health problems.

- An important strategy in reducing stigma is education.

- Ireland has a serious self-harm and suicide problem, with around 11,000 episodes of deliberate self-harm presenting at hospital A&E departments each year and up to 500 suicide deaths reported.

12

Facts and Figures
about Depresson

**"Statistics are human beings
with the tears wiped off"**

PAUL BROEUR

- Over 400,000 people in Ireland experience depression every year. Depression remains an under-reported illness, so the actual figure is thought to be much higher.

- Depression hospitalises approximately 10,000 people in Ireland each year.

- The average number of suicide deaths in Ireland each year is 495 and experts suggest approximately 80 per cent of suicides can be attributed to depression.

- According to the World Health Organisation, by the year 2020, depression will be the *number two* cause of "lost years of health life" worldwide.

- Although women are three to four times more likely than men to suffer from depression, men are far more likely to die by suicide.

- Over 154 million people globally suffer from depression every year *(WHO, 2002)*.

- One in two women and one in four men will experience depression at some time in their lives.

- One in three people will be affected by depression at some point in their lives, either directly or as a family member.

- Depression is among the leading causes of disability worldwide and four of the ten leading causes of disability worldwide are mental disorders *(World Health Organisation)*.

- Three out of four people hide their depression from employers, supervisors, and work colleagues.

- Approximately one in ten of thirteen- to nineteen-year-olds have a depressive disorder.

- A lack of awareness and knowledge about the signs and symptoms of depression means it is an under-reported illness. Some people may suspect they are depressed, but avoid seeking medical advice and/or treatment for fear of being "labelled".

- Globally, nearly 5 to 10 per cent of people in a community at a given time are in need of help for depression *(World Health Organisation)*.

- The stigma that surrounds depression remains a burden to those who are being treated for the illness.

- Depression can occur at any age, but people under forty-five are much more likely to suffer from depression than people over forty-five. This means that the illness is more likely to affect people during the most productive years of their lives *(World Health Organisation)*.

- For every one person who experiences depression directly, as many as five others will be impacted upon. This particularly applies to family members, but also includes close friends.

- Depression crosses all social, religious and cultural divides. It is not more prevalent in any one socio-economic background.

- There are three main types of depression:

  Reactive, which comes about as a reaction to an often traumatic major life event;

  Endogenous, which is due to internal biological factors and can occur after little stress, or indeed after a major life event; and,

  Bi-polar disorder (previously known as manic depression), which involves periods of elation or mania, which alternate with bouts of depression.

- It is generally accepted that children under the age of twelve can develop bipolar disorder.

287

- The Irish suicide rate has doubled since the early 1980s *(Central Statistics Office – CSO)*.

- Suicide is now the single biggest killer of young men aged fifteen to twenty-four and takes more lives in this age bracket than road traffic accidents.

- Suicide is at least four times more common in men than in women *(CSO)*.

- The total number of officially recorded suicides in Ireland in 2004 was 493. The figure for 2005 was 431 deaths, but this figure is based on "year of registration data" (rather than year of occurrence) and is preliminary *(Source: CSO, 2007)*.

- Men under thirty-five years old account for around 40 per cent of all suicide deaths (CSO).

- By the year 2020, depression will be the second largest killer after heart disease and studies show depression is a contributory factor to fatal coronary disease. *(WHO, 10/2001)*.

- Over 11,000 cases of deliberate self-harm are seen in Irish hospitals every year *(National Registry of Deliberate Self-Harm – NRDSH)*.

- Some 21 per cent of deliberate self-harm acts are "repeat acts" *(NRDSH)*. The highest rates of deliberate self-harm are among females aged fifteen to nineteen years *(NRDSH)*.

- Suicide kills more people in the world than war. According to the WHO, approximately 877,000 people die by suicide every year.

- Fewer than 25 per cent of those with depression world wide have access to effective treatments *(World Health Organisation)*.

- As much as 8 to 20 per cent of people carry the risk of developing depression during their lifetime *(World Health Organisation)*.

13

In Good Company

"Culture would be much poorer without the mental
brilliance of those with a mental illness, among
them some of the greatest thinkers, artists,
educators, statesmen of all time."

NATIONAL ASSOCIATION OF MENTAL ILLNESS, WESTERN CAROLINA

Depression affects people from all walks of life and from all backgrounds. It does not discriminate against the rich, the famous or the talented. In fact, some of the most talented, brightest and famous individuals in history are know to have suffered from the "black dog" that is depression. Research shows that writers and poets are far more likely to suffer from affective disorders and, in particular, depression. One study that was carried out in 1994 concentrated on the lives of 291 world-famous men. The results vindicated the belief that depression is far more prevalent than is reported. Over 40 per cent of these men had suffered from some type of depression during their lives, with famous writers being the most prone at 72 per cent. Artists followed these at 42 per cent, politicians at 41 per cent, intellectuals at 36 per cent, composers at 35 per cent and scientists at 33 per cent. Of these famous people who suffered from depression, some responded well to primary treatment, some were hospitalised, some attempted suicide and, sadly, some committed suicide.

There are, however, many famous men and women who have suffered from depression; here is but a small sample.

- *Writers:*

  Samuel Johnson; F. Scott-Fitzgerald, who was hospitalised; Theodore Dostoevsky; Ernest Hemingway, who was hospitalised before committing suicide; Charles Dickens; Leo Tolstoy, author of *War and Peace*, who was struck with depression just after he started writing *Anna Karenina*; Virginia Woolf, who was hospitalised, but went on to take her own life; Truman Capote; and one of my personal favourites, Samuel Beckett. Beckett won the Nobel Prize for Literature in 1969 and was plagued with depression from when he was a young adult, when he would stay in bed for long periods and reject long conversations. His depression frequently showed in his writing, particularly in his masterpiece, *Waiting for Godot* – voted the "most significant English-language play of the twentieth century". The play depicted the struggle to get through life. It was initially written in French, as much of Beckett's work was, but it was one of the few things he translated into English himself. Although he continued to write until his death in 1989, towards the end he remarked that, to him, each word seemed to be "an unnecessary stain on silence and nothingness".

- *Poets:*

  William Blake; Lord Byron; Percy Bysshe Shelley; Vladimir Mayakovsky; Emily Dickinson, who during her lifetime had only seven of her poems published, but left a legacy of over 2,000; T.S. Eliot, who was hospitalised; Edgar Allan Poe, who attempted suicide; Alfred Lord Tennyson; Sylvia Plath; Ted Hughes; and Dylan Thomas, regarded by many as one of the twentieth century's most influential poets.

- *Artists*:

  French Impressionist painter, Claude Monet, who suffered from depression after the death of his wife, Alice Hoschedé; Michelangelo; Ernst Ludwig Kirchner, who was hospitalised before committing suicide; Edvard Munch, most famous for his painting "The Scream". After his father's death he went into a deep depression and, at the age of forty-five, was hospitalised for eight months. Finally, another personal favourite of mine, Vincent Van Gogh, who, in a state of depression, went into a wheat field and shot himself in the chest. He died two days later in the arms of his brother, Theo. Interestingly, Van Gogh's last painting depicted a man sitting with his head in his hands as if he were depressed.

- *Political figures*:

  Sir Winston Churchill suffered from recurring bouts of depression and famously called his depression "Black Dog". Abraham Lincoln, sixteenth President of the United States, battled against depression from

293

his twenties and it continued throughout his life. Menachem Begin, sixth Prime Minister of Israel, whose depression was triggered by the death of his wife. Theodore Roosevelt, twenty-sixth President of the US, suffered from depression throughout his life and had a brother who had to be institutionalised and a son who committed suicide. Roosevelt wrote forty books and is said to have read a book a day, even when he was President.

- *Inventors, Intellectuals and an Astronaut*:

Some of the most brilliant minds in history belonged to individuals who suffered from depression. Among these were: Isaac Newton, commonly referred to as one of the foremost scientific intellects of all time, who had several nervous breakdowns; physicist Stephen Hawking, author of *A Brief History of Time*, who became depressed shortly after being diagnosed with Lou Gehrig's disease and again in 1976 after being hospitalised for medical reasons; Thomas Edison, arguably the world's greatest inventor, whose inventions included the phonograph, the light bulb and the movie camera; Sigmund Freud, psychiatrist and also known as the father of psychoanalysis, who suffered from chronic depression throughout his life; Charles Darwin, explorer and scientist, who is perhaps most known for his theory of evolution, also suffered from depression; finally, astronaut Buzz Aldrin suffered from his first bout of depression shortly after going to the moon with Neil

Armstrong. He was hospitalised, but recovered with a combination of medication and psychotherapy and subsequently wrote about this.

- *Composers:*
Ludwig Von Beethoven had bipolar disorder and wrote some of his most famous works during times of torment. He used opium and alcohol for relief from his symptoms and died of liver disease. Rachmaninoff, Schumann, Mozart, Handel and Tchaikovsky all suffered from affective disorders and Irving Berlin and Cole Porter suffered from depressive illnesses. Robert Schumann was hospitalised and also attempted suicide.

- *Modern well-known people:*
English actor, writer and comedian Stephen Fry famously walked out of the West End play *Cell Mates* in 1995 after just five performances. He was unable to cope with the poor reviews he was getting for his performances. Speaking of his depression, Fry said: "When you get just a complete sense of blackness or void ahead of you, that somehow the future looks an impossible place to be, and the direction you are going seems to have no purpose, there is this word *despair* which is a very awful thing to feel. It was as if I had been in the fast lane without bothering to change oil and with my foot on the accelerator permanently. I was just belting along and various gaskets had to get worn eventually. You convince yourself that you're happy. You say: 'I can't

be miserable because I'm supposedly successful.' But happiness is no respecter of persons." Fry has since undergone therapy and drug treatment for his depression and speaks about his illness quite openly.

- Footballer Stan Collymore has spoken about the hell of his clinical depression, which culminated in him not turning up for an FA Cup match. On the advice of his agent, Collymore sought help at the Priory Clinic. Speaking of his depression, Collymore said: "If I had not gone to the Priory, I could not have guaranteed my next five hours on the planet. I sat at home and I considered suicide because I thought, 'well, what's the alternative?' It's like being in a bubble of nothing. It is as if someone takes your brain out, takes your physical capabilities away. I would pinch myself but I just felt numb. It is hard to describe to someone who is functioning normally what it is to be an emotional void. One in five people in this country suffer from the illness at some stage. It is something you can't really describe unless you go through it. I would not wish it on anybody. It is not a case of just being down. It's a lot more deep-rooted. It disengages you from functioning properly."

- Robbie Williams has struggled with recurring episodes of depression, which have been well documented in the press. American tennis-star and multi-grand slam title winner, Monica Seles, wrote about her depression, which began after she was stabbed in the back in 1993. Singers Elton John and Billy Joel both battled periods of severe depression, with Joel once trying to commit suicide by ingesting furniture polish.

- Famous comedians who have suffered from depression include: Spike Milligan, Peter Sellers, Kenneth Williams, Peter Cook, Billy Connolly, Woody Allen, Jim Carrey, Owen Wilson, Rosie O'Donnell and Roseanne Barr.

- Author J.K. Rowling suffered from depression and had suicidal thoughts before writing her phenomenal *Harry Potter* series of books, according to a report in *The Sunday Times* on 23 March 2008. Rowling revealed that she had thought about killing herself while suffering from depression as a struggling single mother living in a small flat with her daughter. Rowling says she has never been remotely ashamed of suffering from depression and instead says she was proud that she overcame the adversities that caused her depression. She received professional help and now speaks about her mental health problems in an effort to highlight and challenge the stigma that surrounds depressive illness.

14

Getting Well
and Staying Well

"One can have no smaller or greater mastery
than mastery of oneself."

LEONARDO DA VINCI

The road to recovery and returning to normal living can take some adjusting to. I would like to thank Aware for their input and also for permission to use their leaflet: *Continuing your Recovery from Depression: A Guide to Staying Well*, which is reproduced below.

Taking Time

It is important to acknowledge that getting back to old routines will not happen overnight. Dealing with a period of illness is difficult. If you have withdrawn from family and friends as a result of illness, it will take time to rebuild these relationships. Similarly if you have had to take leave from work/school/college it will take some time to adjust to being back in these day-to-day routines.

Do not put pressure on yourself to get back to "normal" straight away. Recovery times vary from person to person: you must go easy on yourself and not put yourself under undue pressure. Ensure you get adequate sleep/rest and that you eat a nutritious diet. Remember that sugary foods lead to a sharp drop in blood sugar levels later on and this leads to slumps in energy and low mood.

Facing Fears and Challenges

It is entirely normal to feel nervous or frightened about the challenges ahead and anxious about returning fully to family life and/or work after a period of ill health. If you are experiencing such feelings, remind yourself that they are normal and very common. Accessing support at this time is crucial. Consider attending an Aware Support Group or using the Aware loCall Helpline (contact details feature at the back of this book).

Tips for Continuing Recovery and Staying Well

- Acknowledge that this is a period of transition and will take time.

- Be kind to yourself.

- Focus on progress you have made so far and remember that recovery always takes time.

- Stay in touch with your doctor or health professional and attend all appointments. If you are required to continue medication, it is essential that you comply with directions – otherwise you may risk relapse.

- Ask family and friends for support. Most will be happy to do what they can to help you through your recovery. Don't be afraid to reach out to them, and don't expect them to read your mind either. If you cannot rely on family support, use the support services Aware offers: the loCall Helpline and support groups.

- Learn what you can about depression so you can monitor movements more readily. Knowing what you are dealing with makes the situation easier to manage.

- When you feel ready, examine old routines and lifestyle choices that may have an impact on your condition. Alcohol and recreational drugs have a detrimental effect on the mood, and this is especially true for individuals prone to mood disorder. If this was the case for you in the past, make a conscious effort to stay away from these substances and to find alternative social outlets where you won't feel under pressure to use them.

- Accessing support services such as those offered by Aware can prove vital, both during recovery and also once full health is regained. Aware support groups offer the opportunity to share concerns and coping skills with others who have personal experience of depression.

- The Aware Helpline is a confidential listening service and offers the opportunity to talk through concerns with a trained volunteer. Even when an individual has fully recovered from a period of illness, it is normal to have concerns from time to time and you should talk these through with someone who understands rather than allow them to develop.

- Many people experience one-off incidents of depression. However, there will be some instances where a subsequent episode will occur. If you are especially concerned about this, consider keeping a mood diary, to plot your mood level on a daily or weekly basis. If you think that you may be relapsing, don't worry about this on your own: talk to someone you trust and see your treating doctor to discuss your concerns. If you haven't already spoken to your GP or health professional, do so now.

(Free information packs on depression are available from Aware. Their address, loCall Helpline number and website are listed at the back of this book.)

References

Avery, D.H., Kizer, D., Bolte, M.A., Hellekson C., "Bright light therapy of subsyndromal seasonal affective disorder in the workplace: morning vs. afternoon exposure", *Acta Psychatrica*, 2001.

Aware, *Continuing your Recovery from Depression, A Guide to Staying Well* (leaflet).

Baldwin, R.C, Chiu, E., Katona, C., Graham, N., *Guidelines on Depression in Older People*, London, Martin Dunitz, 2002.

Beck, A.T., Rush, A.J., Shaw, B.F., Emery, G., *Cognitive Therapy of Depression*, The Guilford Press, 1979.

Brent, DA, Birmaher, B., "Adolescent depression", *New England Journal of Medicine*, 347 (9): 667–671, 2002.

Brink T.L., Yesavage, J.A., Lum, O., Heersema, P., Adey, M.B., Rose, T.L.: "Screening tests for geriatric depression", *Clinical Gerontologist*, 1: 37–44, 1982.

Burke, S., McKeon, P., "Suicide and the reluctance of young men to use mental health services", *Irish Journal Psychological Medicine*, 24(2): 67–70, 2007.

Centre for Addiction and Mental Health, *When a Parent is Depressed . . . What Kids Want to Know*, Centre for Addiction and Mental Health, 2008.

Central Statistics Office, *Principal Statistics,* 2006.

Cochran, S.V., Rabinowitz, F.E., *Men and Depression: Clinical and Empirical Perspectives*, San Diego: Academic Press, 2000.

Colgan, K., *If It Happens To You: Miscarriage & Stillbirth – A Human Insight*, A&A Farmar, 1994.

Colgan, K., *You Have to Scream With Your Mouth Shut: Violence in the Home*, Marino, 1995.

Department of Health and Children, *A Vision for Change: Report of the Expert Group on Mental Health Policy*, Department of Health and Children, Ireland, 2006.

Department of Health and Children and the Health Service Executive, *Reach Out: A National Strategy for Action on Suicide Prevention*, Department of Health and Children and the Health Service Executive, 2005.

Diamond, J., *The Male Menopause*: *Differences Between Male and Female Depression*, Sourcebooks, 1997.

Diamond, J., *The Irritable Male Syndrome: Understanding and Managing the Four Key Causes of Depression and Aggression*, Rodale, 2005.

Effective Health Care, *Improving the recognition and management of depression in primary care*, Volume 7, Number 5, 2002.

Fieve, R., *Mood Swing*, New York, William Morrow, 1989.

Fitzpatrick, C., Sharry, J., *Coping With Depression in Young People*, Wiley, 2004.

Golant, M., Golant, S., *What to Do when Someone You Love is Depressed*, Villard, 1997.

Griest, J.H., James, W., *Depression and its Treatment*, American Psychiatric Press, 1992.

Haley, C., *Stigma* (Talk given at Aware conference), 2005.

Health Service Executive National Office for Suicide Prevention, *Mental Health in Ireland: Awareness and Attitudes*, 2007.

Lewinsohn, P, Gregory, M., Clark, N., et al., "Major depression in community adolescents: Age, episode duration, and time of recurrence", *Journal of the American Academy of Child & Adolescent Psychiatry*, 33 (6): 809, 1994.

Lyons, D., O'Luanaigh, C., O'Dowd, C., Gallagher, J., *Depression in Later Life – A Guide for the Older Person and their Families*, Aware.

Malady, Lucy, *What Do You See?* 2008.

Mangaoang, M.A., Lacey, J.V., "Cognitive rehabilitation: assessment and treatment of persistent memory impairments following ECT", *Advances in Psychiatry*, 13: 90–100, 2007.

McKeon, P., *Depression: The Facts*, Dublin, Aware, 2000.

McKeon, P., Healy, J., Bailey, G., Ward, G., *Depression: Keeping Hope Alive – A Guide for Family and Friends*, Dublin, Aware, 2000.

McKeon, P., Mynett-Johnson, L., Claffey, E., *Prevalence of Depressive Illness in Ireland: A National Survey*, Aware, 1993.

Mental Health Commission, *Annual Report*, 2002.

Mood Disorders Association of Manitoba, *What Do All These Famous People Have in Common?* 1999.

Nairn, C., Smith, G., *Dealing with Depression*, The Women's Press, 2001.

National Suicide Research Foundation, *Young People's Mental Health: A report of the results from the Lifestyle and Coping Survey*, 2004.

Offer, D., Schonert-Reichl, K.A., "Debunking the myths of adolescence. Findings from recent research", *Journal of the American Academy of Child & Adolescent Psychiatry*, 31 (6): 1003, 1992.

O'Hanlon, B., *Stress: The Common Sense Approach*, Newleaf, 1998.

Post, F., "Creativity and psychopathology: A study of 291 world-famous men", *British Journal of Psychiatry*, 165: 22–34, 1994.

Post Natal Depression Ireland, *Changes in Lifestyle*, 2008.

Psychology Information Online, *Women and Depression*, www.psychologyinfo.com

Psychology Today, "Celebrity Meltdown", pp. 46-49, 70, 78, December 1999.

Quinnett, P., *Suicide the Forever Decision, For those Thinking about Suicide and for Those who Know, Love and Counsel Them*, QPR Institute, 1987.

Redfield Jamison, K., *Touched with Fire: Manic-Depressive Illness and the Artistic Temperament*, Maxwell Macmillan International, 1993.

Winokur, G., *Depression: The Facts*, Oxford University Press, 1981.

Witkin, G., *The Female Stress Syndrome*, Newmarket Press, 1991.

Witt, J.A., *When I Am Hurting*, 2008.

Wolpert, L., *Malignant Sadness: The Anatomy of Depression*, London, Faber and Faber, 1999.

World Health Organisation, *By 2020*.

WHO, *Mental Health in the WHO European Region*, Fact sheet EURO/03/03.

World Health Organisation, *Mental Health: New Understanding, New Hope*, 2001.

World Health Organisation, Health Organisation Regional Office for Europe, 2003.

Yesavage, J.A., Brink, T.L., Rose, T.L., Lum, O., Huang, V., Adey, M.B., Leirer, V.O., "Development and validation of a geriatric depression screening scale: A preliminary report" *Journal of Psychiatric Research*, 17: 37–49, 1983.

Further Reading

Brampton, S., *Shoot the Damn Dog*, Bloomsbury, 2008.

Bentley Mays, J., *In the Jaws of the Black Dogs: A Memoir of Depression*, HarperCollins NY, 1999.

Diamond, J., *Inside Out: Becoming My Own Man*, San Raphael, CA: Fifth Wave Press, 1983.

Diamond, J., *The Whole Man Program: Reinvigorating Your Body, Mind and Spirit After Forty*, John Wiley & Sons Inc., 2003.

Diamond, J., *Surviving Male Menopause: A Guide for Women and Men*, Sourcebooks, 2000.

National Office for Suicide Prevention, *Mental Health in Ireland: Awareness and Attitudes* (available as a pdf download from: http://www.nosp.ie/ufiles/news0003/mental-health-in-ireland-awareness-and-attitudes.pdf)

Quinnett, P., *Suicide the Forever Decision, For those Thinking about Suicide and for Those who Know, Love and Counsel Them*, QPR Institute, 1987 (available as a free e-book in pdf format from http://www.hopeline.com/docs/suicide.pdf)

Redfield Jamison, K., *An Unquiet Mind*, Picador, 1997.

Redfield Jamison, K., *The Severity of Depression*, Alfred A. Knopf, 1999.

Redfield Jamison, K., *Exuberance: The Passion for Life*, Alfred A. Knopf, 2004.

Real, T., *I Don't Want To Talk About It*, Gill and Macmillan, 1997.

Solomon, A., *The Noonday Demon*, Chatto & Windus, London, 2001.

Styron, W., *Darkness Visible: A Memoir of Madness*, Knopf Publishing Group, 1990.

Useful Contacts

Aware
72 Lower Leeson Street
Dublin 2
Tel: (01) 661 7211
Fax: (01) 661 7217
Helpline: 1890 303 302
Email: info@aware.ie
Website: www.aware.ie

The Samaritans
112 Marlborough Street
Dublin 1
Tel: 1850 60 90 90 (24-hr)
Email: jo@samaritans.org
Website: www.dublinsamaritans.ie

Mental Health Ireland
6 Adelaide Street
Dun Laoghaire
Co. Dublin
Tel: (01) 284 1166
Fax: (01) 284 1736
Email: via website
Website: www.mentalhealthireland.ie

GROW (Support for sufferers of
mental health problems)
Ormonde Home,
Barrack Street,
Kilkenny
Infoline: 1890 474 474
E-mail: info@grow.ie
Website: www.grow.ie

Irish Association of Suicidology (IAS)
16 New Antrim Street,
Castlebar,
Co. Mayo
Tel: 094 925 0858
Email: info@ias.ie
Website: www.ias.ie

National Office of Suicide Prevention (NOSP)
Dr Steevens' Hospital,
Dublin 8
Tel: (01) 635 2179
Email: info@nosp.ie
Website: www.nosp.ie / www.yourmentalhealth.ie

Post Natal Depression (PND) Ireland
Support line: 021 4923162
(Tue & Thur 10.00 a.m. – 2.00 p.m.)
Email: support@pnd.ie
Website: www.pnd.ie

Friends of the Elderly
25 Bolton Street
Dublin 1
Tel: (01) 873 1855
Email: info@friendsoftheelderly.ie
Website: www.friendsoftheelderly.ie

Childline (An ISPCC Initiative)
29 Lower Baggot Street,
Dublin 2
Telephone: (01) 676 7960
CHILDLINE: 1800 66 66 66
E-mail: ispcc@ispcc.ie

Alone
1 Willie Bermingham Place
Dublin 8
Tel/Fax: (01) 679 1032
Website: www.alone.ie

Useful Websites

www.about-teen-depression.com

www.alone.ie

www.allaboutdepression.com

www.aware.ie

www.camh.net/About_Addiction_Mental_Health/
Mental_Health_Information/when_parent_depressed.html

www.childline.ie

www.dublinsamaritans.ie

www.grow.ie (mental health)

www.depressionalliance.org

www.depressiondialogues.ie

www.friendsoftheelderly.ie

www.ias.ie (Irish Association of Suicidology)

www.irishhealth.com/clin/depression

www.kidshealth.com/teen/your_mind

www.leela.ie (holistic approach)

www.menalive.com (promoting positive male mental health)

www.nomoredepression.org

www.primacare.ie (healthcare group medical / counselling help)

www.pnd.ie (Post Natal Depression Ireland)

www.ppdsupportpage.com (Online PND support group)

www.postpartum.net

www.psychologyinfo.com/depression

www.pinkfridge.com/hab_depression (women's health)

www.readthesigns.org (interactive site for young people aged fourteen to twenty-five)

www.sada.co.uk (Seasonal Affective Disorder Association)

www.teenline.ie

www.stopdepressiontoday.com

www.theblackdog.net (aimed at men)

www.theirritablemale.com

www.youthinmind.net (For stressed youth and those who care for them)

www.webmd.com

www.youth.ie

Notes

Notes

Notes